What people

Happiness: Make

I have been writing books for over twenty-five years now, and have encountered various psychics, mediums and writers throughout that time. I first met Katie in the beginning of 2016, and was blown away by her beautiful heart and loving spirit. Since May 2016, Katie has posted inspirational videos and posts to my Facebook page every week, and has helped thousands of people. I have no doubts in her abilities as a writer, or as an inspirational speaker. She is the angel who gives us all wings to fly!
Theresa Cheung, author

Katie Oman is one of *Chat It's Fate*'s top columnists. She writes with a clarity, but in a beautiful down-to-earth style. Much loved by our readership, people flock to her in droves, seeking her wise and compassionate advice. They trust her – and they're right to.
Mary Bryce, editor of *Chat It's Fate* magazine

So many books out there promise to make you happy. There is a vast array of books proclaiming to 'self'-help yourself to a happy state of mind, and yet, there are still millions upon millions of unhappy people out there. Why is that?

One of the reasons is that no one has ever before written such an accessible book as this one.

Katie's way of writing not only draws you and captures your attention immediately, but from the get-go, you just know this book was written exclusively for you, even though you also know every other reader will feel exactly the same!

Katie just seems to know how you feel, she empathises so well that you could almost have written it all yourself.

Not only that but the tiny bud of confidence the opening chapter gives you grows and grows from that point on.

A lot of books out there leave you feeling like you just can't be bothered, because not being bothered is one of the key symptoms of depression.

Katie's natural sunshine sustains your soul while it sustains your interest, and I guarantee that you will jump on board her happy wagon in no time.

Finally, here is a book that doesn't make you feel inadequate or hopeless, in fact on the contrary your endorphins start multiplying immediately. Let your joy grow as your soul starts to smile!
Jenny Smedley, author

Katie Oman is the real deal. A gifted psychic, intuitive and writer who has lit up the pages of HigherSelfie.co as a regular contributor on numerous occasions. Katie is a fresh bright voice on the spirituality and personal development scene, with her infectious positivity and down-to-earth accessible style. Sometimes you meet a person you know was born to do this, and it simply isn't an option for them to do anything else. Katie is one of those people. We're excited for this next chapter in her journey as we truly believe the world needs her words and her work and we can't wait to read her book.
Lucy Sheridan and **Jo Westwood**, authors of *HigherSelfie*

Reviews

This truly inspiring, thought-provoking and well-written book is an absolute must for everyone – from self-help fans, to everyday women and men of all ages who are seeking to feel more happy, fulfilled and hopeful. Guaranteed to have you gripped – and laughing out loud – from the first page, it features fun, practical and extremely effective techniques you can easily incorporate into your daily life – no matter how busy, tired or stressed you are. Katie's down-to-earth, touchingly honest and witty writing style makes you feel like you're listening to a really close friend. I'd highly recommend it to everyone, and can't wait to read more from her.

Golnaz Alibagi, author

Happiness seems such an elusive state of being these days. Everyone wants it, everyone chases it, but how to get it? Katie delivers the answers to finding happiness in bite-size pieces that are easy to follow and very doable. Scattered with personal stories, glitterbombs, and unicorns *Happiness: Make Your Soul Smile* is a feel-good guide to being authentically happy.

Lyn Thurman, author

I loved the insight that Katie gave me into the first few chapters of her book as to how we can all take charge and change our lives. She writes in a friendly, easy to turn the pages tone which inspires you to read more. I would absolutely love to read more from this talented lady who I think has a lot left to say in the mind, body and spirit market.

Kim Nash, Bookouture, Publicity and Social Media Manager

Happiness:
Make Your Soul Smile

Happiness:
Make Your Soul Smile

Katie Oman

BOOKS

Winchester, UK
Washington, USA

First published by O-Books, 2018
O-Books is an imprint of John Hunt Publishing Ltd., 3 East Street, Alresford, Hampshire
SO24 9EE, UK
office1@jhpbooks.net
www.johnhuntpublishing.com

For distributor details and how to order please visit the 'Ordering' section on our website.

ISBN: 978 1 78535 770 1
978 1 78535 771 8 (ebook)
Library of Congress Control Number: 2017944396

A CIP catalogue record for this book is available from the British Library.

Design: Stuart Davies

Printed and bound by CPI Group (UK) Ltd, Croydon, CR0 4YY, UK

We operate a distinctive and ethical publishing philosophy in
all areas of our business, from our global network of authors to
production and worldwide distribution.

Contents

Dedicated to every single person on this big, beautiful planet. Buckets of love to you all.

So, here's the thing...

We need to talk.

Ooo... there's a sentence you never want to hear. That tricky little sentence normally strikes fear into the hearts of everyone that hears it, right? Four little words that normally lead to break-ups, dark secrets being revealed, and a shedload of nastiness.

Don't panic, this is a positive book.

What we do need to talk about is...

Happiness!

I believe happiness is one of the most powerful, awesome, and magical energies in the whole cosmos, and it's time we got some of this for ourselves. After all, it's the thing we all want most in life, isn't it? The thing we all chase, the purpose behind every word, deed and wish. We all want to be happy. And I'll let you into a little secret: come closer... that's it... let me whisper in your ear –

Happiness is chasing you too!

Look, I know it doesn't feel like that. I know that most of the time life can feel tough and unfair; especially in our modern world. It sometimes feels as though every media outlet seems to be a competitor in a never-ending competition that has never actually been officially announced. The *'Let's Scare the Crap Out of Everyone at Every Given Turn'* competition. Whether it's the TV news, panel shows, newspapers or Internet – the whole media brigade seems to be on a non-stop mission to highlight the fear that's seemingly all around us. And do you know what? I've had enough. I'm tired of being scared all the time. Tired of being suspicious of others, and tired of letting fear rule my life.

Surely there has to be a better way? I don't know about you, but I've had enough of this consistent fear mongering. I'm tired of being afraid of the world, and worrying about worst-case scenarios all the time. And I'm tired of being made to feel that those who are different to me are somehow bad or someone I have to worry about. I for one don't want to live my life like this. I'm not naïve or daft by the way; I know terrible things *do* happen in the world every day. Unimaginable horrors that can shake you to your very core. I'm not suggesting that we stick our fingers in our ears and all live in a land of rainbows and sunshine. All I am simply saying is that we are out of balance with the world, and the way we have been trying to cope with things clearly hasn't been working. A new way is desperately needed, lest things get any worse.

Neither am I walking around with my eyes closed to what's really happening out there. The world *can* be a really scary place at times. There are things happening in the world so far off the scale of unfair and wrong, it's downright terrifying. All I *am* saying is the way we are trying to deal with things clearly isn't working. This fight mentality we all have of rolling up our sleeves and declaring war on anything that makes us feel scared is only bringing more of the same to our proverbial front door. The minute you engage in any kind of battle like this, you're simply bringing more fear energy into your life. Hence why we're all scuttling around like wide-eyed rabbits, all afraid of our own shadows. This book is not a magic wand to wave over it all and make all that darkness disappear. How I wish I could do that for you! This book is attempting to restore some sense of balance within your own mind; to help you see that, despite the perceived saturation of fear in the world, you can still have happiness in your own life. Goodness knows you deserve it; we all do!

I know that sometimes, when you're stuck in the depths of fear and crap, it can seem as if happiness has lost your contact details, and won't be getting in touch anytime soon. But, I need you to understand that things aren't as grim as they may appear. Happiness is your birthright – you deserve to be happy, and you're worthy of it too. You don't have to be a certain age, gender, weight, or have a certain job. You don't need to be attracted to particular people, or have a body that's 'normal'. There really are no special criteria that determine whether you deserve to be happy or not. Simply by the fact you're alive… that's it! You have the right to be happy because you are here on planet Earth right now.

Everyone take a deep breath. Isn't a huge relief to be told that? But…

Yes, there's another 'but' here. I'm sorry, I didn't want to put one in either, but needs must and this has to be said. So, bear with me for a minute, and we'll get back to the super happy, high-fiving mode in a second. Promise.

Happiness is a conscious choice you've got to make every single day. Granted, there are going to be times in your life where you can't stop smiling because life feels so wonderfully incredible, but there will also be times when life is a bit more, well… crap. Days when you can't pull up your inner sunshine from your soul no matter how much you want to, and the world feels nothing but mean/hard work/boring (delete as appropriate).

At times like that it may be hard to acknowledge that you deserve to be happy. Indeed, in that moment, it probably feels like you've sent happiness a friend request on Facebook. Not only did it ignore you, but it's permanently blocked you, and reported you to boot. This book may feel like a smug 'oh-look-at-me-and-how-happy-I-am' slap around the face from me if you're in this place in your life, but nothing could be further from the truth. I'm not happy all the time, despite assumptions to the contrary. I don't go skipping through fields of rainbows and sunshine, hand in hand with my pet unicorn. Oh, that life were that easy.

My day starts out happy enough. I wake up in the morning and I visualise myself having a good day. I see everything running smoothly, and I picture myself with the biggest smile on my face. Not only this, but I always set my intentions for the day. I do this by focusing on how I want to feel throughout the day. It could be loved, happy, nurtured, or even like the true spiritual rock-star goddess that I am! By setting this intention at the beginning of my day, it gives me an inner guidance system that I can then align all my choices with throughout the next 24 hours; like a spiritual GPS. Let me give you an example – let's say I'm feeling hormonal, and full of crappy that-time-of-the-month ickiness. In that moment, I am tempted to consume my body weight in chocolate; enough cocoa to sink an aircraft carrier. But my intention for that day was to nurture myself. I know eating several pounds of chocolate may make me happy for a nanosecond, but it'll ultimately lead to feelings of nausea, shame, guilt, and weight gain – none of which hardly meet the criteria for a nurturing kind of day. I would never deny myself chocolate (that's the path to misery, my friends, don't go there), but it's all about balance. Buy one chocolate bar, rather than several.

Anyway, I digress. As I was saying before I got distracted by the brown, sticky yumminess of chocolate, I wanted to show you how my day starts with generally feeling pretty happy. I deliberately focus on raising the happiness levels in my own head by my words, intentions and visualisations. By the time I come to get the children out of bed, I'm normally feeling quite smiley. Shame it doesn't last...

At the time of writing my three children are 14 and 4 (I have twins). I have to get myself and all three of them out of the door by 8:15am. Sounds easy you say? You clearly don't have young children! By the time I leave the house most mornings I have magically transformed from serene goddess of happiness and positivity into a stressed-out banshee of stress who would frighten small children (just ask my kids). All in the space of 1 hour and 15 minutes. Believe me, I'm not centred in my happy bubble all the time; life has a nasty habit of getting in the way.

But... (There's that word again.)

Years ago, I would've stayed in that stressed-out mood for the rest of the day. The manic hour would've left its fingerprints all over me and I wouldn't be able to shake them off. I would allow it to dictate how I felt, even though the event had passed. I couldn't change it, but I gave it power to spoil the rest of my day. It would've had a nasty impact on every relationship I had throughout the day, and the stressed feeling would've made me anxious and unsettled hours after the initial kick up the bum. Not good, and definitely not a strong foundation for lasting happiness.

I now take time to come back to my intentions, to choose happiness again. It may mean sticking some uplifting songs on to lift my mood, or to talk to trusted loved ones who help me get some perspective (and help me see the funny side). Coming back to my happiness is the best strategy to deciding to have a good day, every single day. Some days it may be harder than others to come back, but I always get there. Happiness is too precious, too wonderful, not to want it for yourself. Most of the time it's not going to fall magically in your lap, but you can ignite its spark through the choices you make, and I'm going to help you do just that.

For, when all is said and done, you are not at the mercy of your mind. You have never been a slave to your thoughts, with no power to choose how you feel. As Glinda the Good Witch so eloquently states in the classic film *The Wizard of Oz*:

You've always had the power, my dear, you just had to learn it for yourself.

Anytime you find yourself feeling stuck in negativity of any kind, know that it doesn't have to be that way! You have the power within you to choose another thought; one of happiness and positivity. It's not always easy, granted. Your mind will fight back harder than a cat trapped in a corner at first, but the more you practise and want it, the easier it'll become for you. This book will be a tool of joy to help you along your way. If you are looking for a lift out of the gloom or a light in the darkness, this book will shine brightly for you. For truly, we all deserve nothing less.

So, you may be wondering what this book actually covers? After all, my claims and infectious positivity may sound exciting, but they're hardly going to set your world alight on their own. You'll be happy to know that there's more to this book than vague promises… much, much more! Firstly, we are going to be exploring the uniqueness and beauty that is you! I'm going to show you why you need to stop trying to be like everyone else and start embracing yourself just as you are. There's not much use trying to get happy for you if you're too busy worrying what everyone else is doing now, is there?

From this loving kick up the bum, I'm going to explain how you can find something in every single day to help switch your mind to a more positive setting. And it doesn't have to be the life changing, big stuff either! Yes, those moments are gold dust and should be cherished for what they are, but it's actually when you start noticing the little miracles in each day that you start to become more positive. But, don't worry your head about that right now, I'll explain more when we get there, plus there's my own personal list of happiness to inspire you to find your own moments too. This then moves on to some wonderful ideas that I've personally tried myself to bring happiness into my life in a tangible way. These magical practices will bring much light into your life, and I'll run through everything you need to know to make them a reality.

The next key section of the book is a focus on one of my favourite things: gratitude. I will explain how training your own mind to become more grateful can actually lead you to find an abundance of happiness! I should note that when I say the word 'training', I'm not asking for you to head off to college or anything. This is something that will become part of your daily practice, but it's an easy one to incorporate, and I will show you how. You'll be beyond grateful that you did!

This is an incredibly positive and affirming read, but I am going to focus on five key things that we all engage with that are actually stopping us from being happy: trying to please everyone, fearing change, living in the past, putting yourself down, and overthinking. Each one is going to be explored in turn, and then I'm going to show you how you can flip these bad boys around to create a happier and more peaceful place to be. Believe me, once you've read this section you'll feel as though a huge weight will have been lifted from your shoulders; it's like a tonic for the soul!

The next section of the book is like I'm reaching through the pages to give you a big loving hug. I'm going to show you why it's vital for you to start believing in yourself. This chapter is very personal, and I'll show you what happens when you fall down the rabbit hole of not believing in yourself. As well as the anecdotes, I will give you key tips and advice that you can use to start believing in you. We are on this journey together after all, and you'll soon see that reclaiming happiness has been (and still is) something I've worked through. My hope is, through revealing my own experiences, you'll be able to see that there is a light at the end of the tunnel. Mind, I did get tired of waiting for it, so I lit up the darkness myself (I can be a determined little minx when I want to be)!

Many people seemed to have developed the bad habit of putting off their happiness for some magical future time where they think everything will be perfect, but the next section will show how you can be happy right now! By focusing on the concept of mindfulness, I will examine how you can really start to live in the present moment and how, by doing so, you can shift your focus to start making your life one of happiness and fulfilment rather than wandering off into anxiety. There's a special gift for you to explore at the end of this section: I will explain why music can really help to create happiness for you, and then I'll give you my own happy playlist as inspiration for you to create your own.

An important and lovely practice to help you become happier is kindness, and I will explore why this is such a key tool to work with. Alongside this, I will also give ideas that you could potentially start to work with in your own life. Not only will this help to make you happier, but you'll also be helping to lift others up as well! When the light from a candle is shared, the light from the original source is not dimmed. In the same way, kindness is a gift to all, and it's a practice that I can't emphasise enough. Even if I rolled it in glitter and had it riding into your life on your own personal unicorn!

There's a place that can keep you stuck firmer than a moose in a glue spillage. What is this strange place? The comfort zone! And I will be exploring how, although this place can seem familiar and safe, it actually holds you back in so many ways. I will help you to break out from the sticky place, so that you can start to be the master (or mistress) of your own destiny. Alongside this, I'll set all the lights on the fact that many of us (myself included) are not great at being the assertive force of nature we sometimes need to be, or having clear and defined boundaries. But these are key in helping to establish you as being happy, and I'm going to share some exercises with you that will give you your power back; She-Ra style! (Cue 80s nostalgia moment...)

It's easy to love the parts of yourself that you perceive to be the more positive aspects of the self, but the seemingly negative parts need some loving too. I'm going to take a nosedive into the shadow side of self, and help you to give it all a big squishy hug in the process. Yes, it may not be the most comfortable section in the book, but do you know what? I guarantee it's the one that's going to truly send shockwaves through your life, and set you on the path of establishing some long-lasting happiness. I'm also going to be looking at something truly shocking... it's okay not to be happy all the time. I know that may sound strange in a book that's all about getting happy, but it'll become crystal clear when we get there; promise.

We all have stories we tell others and ourselves about who we are and the lives we have lived up to this point, but these stories can actually stop you from living a life of love, abundance and happiness. I'm going to show you that stories are just perception, and how you really do have the power to write a new story of happiness for yourself in every moment. Not only this, but it's time for a close up and personal look at how we are all drawn to drama in some way. It is a natural part of who we are, but when it starts to become bordering on obsessive it can really suck the happiness out of you. I can show you how you can start to withdraw yourself from being overly connected to drama, so you can make room for happiness in your life instead.

There are two more key elements you may not have realised are important for helping you to become happier: non-attachment and forgiveness. Both are essential for helping you to live a happier and more fulfilled life. Both issues are going to be examined to show how they can pull you down if you don't welcome them into your life, before showing how you can start to really utilise them to bring untold benefits.

It's easy to see failure as the end of the world, as well as taking it really personally, but this mindset doesn't do anyone any favours. Instead, it may be possible that you weren't meant to head down that path, and there's something better in store. This is the focus of this next section of the book, and I will show you how sometimes it's better for you to go with the natural flow of life, rather than fighting it every step of the way. Let's be honest anyway, having a permanent fight mentality is beyond exhausting, and I can certainly think of better ways to spend my time. How can anyone have the energy to focus on being happy if you're too busy trying to make life fit into the perfectly-shaped box you'd picked out specially? Life is full of twists, turns and surprises, and I will help you to accept this more than you may have ever done before.

Self-care has become something of a buzzword in modern life, but many people are still resistant to the idea; or may not even fully understand what it means! The concept of self-care, the different aspects of it, and how it can really bring happiness into your life are the focuses of the next section. I know it's something

I've struggled to bring into my life at times, but when I do I feel myself smiling from head to toe, and I aim to give you the same beautiful gift for your own life. By the same token, I have found a great many people have issues around money that stop them living a full and happy life. These issues are going to be examined in turn, before considering how you can turn your core beliefs about money around to something much more positive.

Relationships are another key factor in all of our lives, but they can also bring the biggest fears and heartache. The next section considers why relationships are actually our biggest teacher in life about what happiness really means, and how you can help to make each of your relationships a healthier and happier place to be, regardless of whether it's with a partner, friend, family member or colleague. And, speaking of key factors – why we are here is one of the biggest life questions we all ponder at some point. We all like to think that we are here for some greater purpose, but this thought can also lead many to end up with untold fear and anxiety. I will examine what the true purpose of life is, and how you can use this knowledge to move towards a life more closely aligned to what your purpose may be.

Finally, the book concludes by summarising each of the key points that have been covered, so the important messages are really highlighted for you to take away and use in your own life. Ultimately, this is your life, and you should spend it being as happy as you can.

Sound good? You ready to set your facial muscles to the smile position? Ready to get your happy on?

Let's do this!

I deserve to be happy!

Stand in Your Own Spotlight

Can we just pause for a second to look at the true miracle that is YOU!

Do you realise there has never been anyone like you in the whole history of the world, and there never will be?

You are a snowflake. Breathtakingly beautiful in your own uniqueness.

You are a fingerprint. Totally original in design.

Do you realise how remarkable that is? There are literally billions of people on this incredible planet we all share, and every single one of them is an extraordinary one-off. Even if you have an identical twin, seemingly alike in every way, you'll still have your own incredible set of traits, quirks and thoughts that make you totally singular in who you are. What a gift that is!

I think some of the problem stems from the fact you see yourself every day. You've become so acclimatised to who you are, the shine has worn off. It's hard to see just how amazing you are when you're not looking at yourself with fresh eyes. That's why it's easier for others to point out our beauty (inner and outer) than it is for us to see it for ourselves. That and the fact we're all carrying around a suitcase full of issues that weighs us down (more on that later). It's easier to look to others to be the shiny and sparkly examples of awesomeness we seek to be, rather than turning up the dimmer switch on our own light.

We need to stop trying to be a sheep in this life (sheep are lovely creatures by the by, and I have nothing against them as animals). If you're a sheep in your own life, it means you're not comfortable in your own skin. You're not celebrating the amazing person you are! You are so wibbly wobbly in your own individuality, you'd rather spend your time following others who you deem to be more special than you.

(Sigh.)

I can't stress enough how special you are just by being you. I don't care if someone else is a star, or has more money than you, or anything else which seems to raise them above the rest of us. Whatever someone else may or may not have does not make them better than you for even a millisecond. If you're the Queen or a beggar, you are a beautiful and amazing person because you are you.

And those who do seek to be a follower rather than standing in their own spotlight ultimately end up lost, unfulfilled and disenchanted. The ones who you see as better than you may do something that proves them to be more human than godly. Their pedestal becomes shaky, but it's you that has placed them upon it. When this happens, the entire way you view the world becomes shaken, and thus makes the way you see yourself also on less than solid ground. By having acceptance and love for yourself, just the way you are, you won't have the same expectations of those around you. You can be you, and you'll let them be who they are: human beings all doing our best to make it through this crazy dance called LIFE.

Followers apologise for who they are. As if the fact they take up space by their sheer existence is a reason to say 'sorry'. They apologise for everything too! Even when it's not their fault. They can't stop themselves because it's all about hiding their light and playing small. If they keep apologising, then others around them may like their light or bypass it altogether. Trouble is, no one ever got truly happy by sending out the sorry signal (kind of like the Batman signal, but a lot less fabulous). If you're apologising continuously then you're sending out the message that you are less than and not worthy of everything you deserve. Mr Sorry and Little Miss Apologise are doing nothing but undermining their self-worth and self-esteem over and over again, even if they're not aware of the part they play in pulling themselves down. So, whether you're doing it to be a people pleaser, or to fill in awkward gaps in social interactions, over-apologising is a huge no-no to happiness.

Don't get me wrong, if you've done something that needs you to say sorry to make amends, then go for it. Taking responsibility for your actions and healing hurt relationships is a healthy practice to bring into your life. But don't be throwing sorry around like confetti at a party; save it for special occasions instead. It'll mean more if you do.

So, let's all stop being sheep. Stop expecting others to lift us up, simply by standing in their light. Stop apologising for existing, saying sorry for who we are. Standing in your own spotlight may not be the easiest thing for you to do. You may feel shy and scared to let the magnificent being that is you shine forth in all its glory, but you don't need to do it all in one go. I'm not asking you to go from pitch black to a 1,000-watt bulb with one switch; you'd be like the literal rabbit caught in the headlights! All I'm asking you to consider is the crazy fact that you matter.

That you are not a waste of space.

You are here for a reason, even if you haven't figured out what that is yet.

You are alive, here on Earth to live your life.

You have dreams, hopes and fears.

You have a loving heart, a compassionate soul and a kind mind.

You have stardust in your bones, and magic in your spirit.

Yes, I'm talking to you.

Let that all sink in for a few seconds... and turn up your light a little brighter.

There is sunshine in my soul today!

Things to Smile About

There are literally thousands of reasons in the world to be happy, but sometimes we go around in our own cloak of misery so we can't see them. Maybe it's because we're waiting for the big, grab you by your collar moments – the lottery wins, the fairy-tale endings. But the wonderful thing about life is it's actually the moments dotted throughout each day that can really lift you up. The smaller things may be so taken for granted they seem insignificant. When you start to simply notice each magical moment, you feel your heart start to samba with happiness!

Let me share my list with you, so you get an idea of what I mean:

Things That Make Me Happy: A List

1. My three beautiful children. Cuddles, playing, joking around – they make me beam with pure, undiluted joy.
2. Uplifting songs. I love music that feels wrapped up in sunshine.
3. Books. I mean the old-fashioned, made from paper type ones too. I love technology, but there's nothing like the feel and smell of a new book, and e-readers just don't have the same magic for me.
4. Bookshops. A place of sheer joy.
5. Libraries. A gift to us all.
6. Making other people laugh. I love clowning around and making an idiot of myself if it makes others happy. Hearing the laughter of those around you is worth the seconds of embarrassment you may feel from being silly.
7. Chocolate. Ooo, I LOVE chocolate in all forms more than words can say! Whether it's milk, dark or white – a good dose of cocoa puts the smile on my face.
8. Learning. There's nothing quite like the feeling of feeling

yourself growing and developing through learning something new. The world is a deeply fascinating place, and there's so much to explore. We never know everything, and being open to fresh ideas is a wonderful way to expand your understanding.

9. Doing an act of kindness for someone else. It doesn't matter if you get something in return or not – seeing someone else light up because you've opened your heart to them is a true blessing we can give every day. Acts of kindness don't have to be mega in terms of cost to you, but they will mean the world to the person on the receiving end. Allow compassion to flow freely, and feel your heart bubble with happiness.

10. Dancing. If you're a talented performer or more of baby deer on ice, there's something joyous in losing yourself in dance. Moving your body to music is a real freedom that will always make your happy centres light up. For me, I don't need an excuse to shake my thang. If there's music playing, I'm grooving!

11. Seeing the leaves change colour in the autumn. Witnessing nature's very own fireworks never loses its appeal. Year after year I find myself watching in awe as the vibrant tones of reds, yellows and oranges burst into form.

12. Talking with my mum. My mum is the one person who knows me upside down, back to front and inside out. She knows how I'm feeling without me saying a word, and is truly the most inspiring, caring and loving person I know. Plus, we have the same sense of humour, which has led to many a happy moment of giggling!

13. Christmas lights. It's easy to become cynical at the commercialisation of Christmas, and the way we're all targeted earlier and earlier to part with our cash, but there's also something magical about this holiday. Seeing the fairy lights twinkling away makes my inner child clap her hands together in glee.

14. A huge big bubble bath. Every time I relax into the hot water I feel all my stresses melt away. Having a relaxing bath is a real treat and one that never goes unappreciated.

15. Letting my inner child out to play. I am a big kid at heart and I always will be. Whether it's colouring, watching cartoons or playing in the park with the kids, I'm truly happy when I allow that part of myself to have real freedom. Just because you're a grown-up doesn't mean you have to be boring and sensible you know!

16. Sitting on a beach. There's something innately very soothing being near the ocean. Watching the waves crash on the shore and hearing the sounds of that magical place is akin to Heaven on Earth.

17. Star and cloud gazing. Looking up into the sky at any time makes me fully appreciate the wonder of nature and my part within it. Whether it's making shapes out of the clouds as they roll lazily by, or seeing the stars winking down at me, looking up always makes me feel happy.

18. Glitter. You can never have too much sparkle, in my opinion. It makes everything feel magical, and adds some much-needed delight to the world.

19. My friends. Whether in person or through the magic of social media (Facebook can be such a magical place), I'm truly grateful for the special people who encourage me, support me, lift me up and make me smile. Each and every one is a gift.

20. Listening to the sounds of a thunderstorm or the rain whilst you're all warm inside with no place to go. Two of the most spine-tingling sounds in nature.

21. Good comedy shows on TV. Whether it's *Friends* (my all-time fave), *The Simpsons*, *Mrs Brown's Boys*, *The Last Leg* or *Russell Howard's Good News* – watching quality comedy always lifts me right up. Nothing like laughing so hard your eyes start leaking happy tears.

22. New stationery. Makes you feel as though you're back in school. Anyone else do their very best handwriting on the first page of a new notebook?
23. Friendly cats and dogs that want to come and say hello. Feels as though you're making a new friend every time.
24. Getting into a bed that has fresh clean sheets. Feels SO good!
25. Rainbows. I would paint the entire world in vivid rainbows if I could; the more colour the better. Rainbows are real magical wonders that always make me smile.
26. The Muppets. This one doesn't need explaining... they're The Muppets, what else needs to be said?!?

That's just my list, but I'm sure you have your own. What's lighting up your day today? Start to notice the things that make you feel deliciously good, and aim to bring more of them into your life. Let's make each day one of magic, joy and covered in rainbow-coloured glitter!

And, while we're at it, I want to let you all into one of the greatest and most underrated tricks to feeling happy: smiling! Don't believe me? Stand in front of a mirror and smile at yourself for at least five seconds. I promise you that you'll probably end up feeling embarrassed and bursting out laughing at your own silly face; but you certainly feel happier, don't you?

The brain is a computer, but one that needs to be programmed to be efficient and of high quality. It literally feedbacks to you what you've inputted into it. So, if you continually tell yourself you're miserable, guess what? You will be! And so it follows that telling yourself you're happy through smiling leads you to feel happier; even if it's a fake one. So, get your facial muscles pointed to the smile position, and watch the sunshine drift from behind the clouds of your life.

I just awesomed
all over the
place!

Here's an Idea…

Buy yourself a lovely jar and decorate it to make it look lovely. Every day write down one thing that has made you really happy and add it to the jar. It doesn't matter if the thing you write about is something huge (marriage, babies, passing exams or moving house) or something small (hey, never knock a good cup of coffee!). Just choose one thing that has put a beautiful smile on your face that day. Do this for one whole year.

At the end of the year, open the jar and read through them to remind you of the amazing things that have happened to you.

The Happiness Jar is a wonderful way to lift you right up and make you see how truly blessed you are!

Or how about a Letter of Thanks? Expressing our gratitude to others can significantly boost our happiness. It can also have a powerful effect on the person on the receiving end, and help strengthen your relationship with them.

So, who are you really grateful to?

Think of three people who have been a really positive influence in your life and for whom you feel really grateful to. They could be a member of your family, an old teacher, long-lost friend, colleague or someone else who has made a real difference in your life. Then, choose one of these people to write to and tell them how grateful you are for everything they have done for you. Maybe it's someone you've not thanked properly before, even though you've always meant to; this is your chance!

Think about the impact this person has had on your life, and write a letter to tell them:

- What specifically are you grateful for from them?
- How have they helped you?
- How did their help make you the person you are today?

You can write the letter any way you like; be as creative as you feel drawn to. The most important thing is to be really linked to your gratitude as you write, and to lead from the heart. You could also arrange to visit the person and read the letter aloud to them. Or maybe post or email the letter, which can be followed up with a phone call.

One of the most effective tools for me has been to create a vision board. This is a visual stimulus that you place in a prominent position to have a constant reminder of your dreams and aspirations. I take an A3 piece of paper and card, and then spend a great deal of time choosing relevant pictures and quotes out of magazines to cut and stick on to it. I have created one several times as my goals have changed along the way, and it's one of the most satisfying and powerful tools in my arsenal. Any aid you create yourself is infused with your own powerful energy, and this in itself can provide a huge sprinkling of magic over making your dreams come true. Having a daily visual reminder is a huge gift to yourself too – it keeps your mind focused on making those dreams a reality.

The final tool I want to share with you (for now) is the power of visualisation. See, it's all well and good thinking about your happiness, and the dreams that will help move you to where you want to be, but when you bring in visualisation it's like stepping the car into hyperdrive! You may have guessed that I'm a very visual kind of person, plus I'm an overthinker; going off into my head and creating strong visual images is part and parcel of what I do anyway!

To work with visualisation, first of all you have to decide what it is you really want to manifest in your life right now. A new job perhaps? A wonderful new romance? Your dream home? Whatever it is that's calling to you, it's time to get your detailed visual caps on. It's best to choose just one thing to focus on for this by the by, just so that you can create a really detailed mental image. Bringing in everything can potentially water down the power that you create by doing this.

Once you've chosen the focus, then it's time to visualise. Ensure you have a quiet spot where you're not going to be disturbed by people or technology for at least 10 minutes. Lock the doors if you have to! Close your eyes and take several deep breaths, all the way down into your belly. Then, imagine yourself in the situation that you want to manifest for yourself. Say, for example, you want to move house. Imagine yourself in the new property. It's really important with visualisation to see as much detail as possible. What colour are the walls? What view can you see out of the window? What can you hear? What can you smell? Adding details like this makes the images more real, and helps your mind to fully accept what it is you are creating.

The other vital part behind this exercise is the emotions. Don't just see the images, but really focus on how you will feel once they become true in real life – excited, happy, and proud. Don't just name them and move on, but allow yourself to fully feel them as you are moving around your visualisation. The more detail you can add to the image, in terms of what you can see and how you will feel, the more power you are whipping up as a whole.

When you feel ready, it's time to release this out into the Universe! Hold your hands out in front of you with your palms facing upwards. Say the words (either aloud or within your mind), 'I surrender!' See your visualisation in a balloon, floating upwards towards the sky. Let it go. You have given it to the Universe now, in as much detail as you possibly can. You now have to have faith that the Universe will provide your dreams into your reality. You won't know when or how it's going to happen, but you can trust that they will! Don't sit back now and be a passive procrastinator though. Start to make things happen! If you want to move house, visit some estate agents, or buy the local paper. Show the Universe that you are serious about this dream, and follow any intuitive guidance that points you in the right direction. This is the Universe talking to you and leading you to where you want to be. Know that everything will be delivered to you at the right time. The power is within you!

Engaging in hands-on activities like these helps to make the happiness train one of fun and engagement. Reading about it is one thing, but doing things where you can see and feel real results will keep you motivated. Never be afraid to put your happiness into practice, and spread the smiles far and wide.

It's a good day to have a good day!

Get Your Gratitude Groove On

There's magic within you that leads to happiness. I want you to gently wave your fairy wand and say the magic words with me. You ready? 1... 2... 3...

I AM GRATEFUL!

Getting your gratitude groove on has become a fashionable buzzword, but it really works! By consciously shifting your thoughts every day to focus on what makes you feel blessed and happy, you will create so many positives for yourself. Like what, I hear you cry! Well, here's just a few to whet your appetite:

- Improved sleep
- Increased energy
- More optimistic
- Improved self-esteem
- Better able to cope with stress
- Better overall health
- Better relationships
- Increased work productivity

Need I go on?

Hey, we're all A+ students at focusing on our problems! We can moan and complain until the cows come home (where do those cows go every day?), but do you take the same time and energy to focus on the good stuff? You know, the things that make you happier than a kangaroo on a trampoline?

So, here's the idea...

At the end of each day, spend around 5 minutes thinking back over the last 24 hours and try to remember the good stuff rather than the bad. Then, write down 3 things you were grateful for that day. It's really important that you do the writing down bit, because it makes the gratitude a more solid thing inside your head.

And it doesn't have to be big stuff either! I mean yes, if you have had the kind of sparkly, kick ass day dreams are made of, then get that bad boy written down! But, if your day was a bit quieter, there's still good stuff to be found. Even if you've had a real crappity crap day, I promise you that you can find moments of sunshine if you really look for them.

Need some inspiration? Here's a very gorgeous list of the smaller moments in life that bring a yummy happiness to my soul:

- A really good cup of coffee
- Feeling the sunshine on my face
- When your hair goes perfect (for a change)
- Someone holding the door open for you when your hands are full
- Getting that perfect parking space
- Laughing until your belly hurts
- Hearing children laughing
- Finding money you'd forgotten about in your bag or coat
- When the Wi-Fi is running at super speed (slow speed is such a d-r-a-g)
- When you hit all green lights on your drive home
- Getting the last biscuit or chocolate in the box and it's a really good one
- Kicking autumnal leaves with big comfy boots on your feet
- The first step on to the beach and feeling the warm sand squidging between your toes
- The smell of cake baking in the oven

And, let me put this to you – there are things that we take for granted so much, we stop noticing what a blessing they are *at all*. The fact that you can see for example. I mean, what an amazing thing it is that you get to witness life in all its beauty and vivid technicolour every day! This ability is denied to so many people, and should be appreciated for the miracle it is. And, while we're on that note, we need to talk about hearing too. Imagine not being able to hear the voices of those you care about, or even the sweet sound of the birds singing you along your way. Your five senses are the most incredible gift, but mostly taken for granted until something goes wrong with them. Give yours some love and gratitude today – just take a moment to be completely mindful. Take in your environment right now where you are. What can you see, hear, smell, taste and feel? What an amazing world we all live in!

Going even further than that, let's take a moment to amaze at the wonder that is your heart, your body and your mind. Your heart pumps away every second of every day, all to keep you alive. The average adult human heart beats 72 times a minute. That works out to be 100,000 times a day; 3,600,000 times a year; and 2.5 billion times during a lifetime! Add to this the fact that your lungs continually draw in oxygen without you even needing to think about doing it, that you have a body that supports you, fights off infection, and continually seeks to help you, and you really are a living miracle! Do you realise what an incredible machine your body is? Everything your body does is to help you be all you can be – talk about true love! So many have bodies that do not function entirely as they should, but every single person upon the Earth is a wonder, a miracle and a gift. We all have things about us that make us unique and incredible. It's time to take a look in the mirror and give real thanks to your body, to your mind, and to yourself. You, my beautiful angel, are one of the true wonders of nature.

Just a few ideas for you to consider. I can't recommend slipping into the gratitude groove enough. It's like holding a magic key that unlocks your happiness door, each and every day! Remember:

It is not happy people who are thankful,

It is thankful people who are happy!

Don't let anyone
dull your sparkle
-
honey, you were
born to shine!

Things You Should Give Up Right Now
(I mean it!)

This is a book all about being happier, and I certainly don't want to bring you down. Chances are, you were looking to turn that frown upside down when you picked up this book, so who am I to add to the murkiness of misery? But, listen up – the things that are listed below are majorly bringing you down in a BIG way. Take it from someone who literally has been there, done it and plastered her bedroom with posters of it (I always did have to go that step further). These are things that we need to chuck out right now, because you don't deserve to spend a second longer with these notorious happiness drainers. What are they? Glad you asked:

- Trying to please everyone
- Fearing change
- Living in the past
- Putting yourself down
- Overthinking

Hands up if you're letting these gremlins into your life...

(I've got both hands raised in the air. Both legs too. Good job this isn't a pop-up book or you'd get more than you bargained for.)

Listen, I know better than anyone how these things can get a grip on you and stop you living the life you deserve; a lifetime of low self-esteem will do that to you. But I realised that I needed to send each one up in its own rocket-fuelled balloon to the ends of space; and you have to jetpack them off too! Do you want to know what these murky monsters will do to you? Let's examine each one in turn (don't worry, we're not going to get bogged down in misery), then I can show you how to flip-flop them into something much more positive!

Trying to please everyone

When you are a chronic people pleaser, you try to keep everyone happy around you at all costs to ensure they like you. Living like this will do you no favours, for when you're overly focused on what others want, you become totally out of sync with your own wants and needs. Helping other people is a great way to boost your own happiness, as well as the person on the receiving end of your help, but there's a huge difference between helping someone and trying to please them. Typically, being a people pleaser centres around an awful lot of assumptions and guesswork concerning what makes others happy, and we then act in accordance to what we think they want. Being a people pleaser seems to be all about the person you're trying to make happy, but actually it's a subtle attempt to manipulate how others see and feel about you. It also removes you from your own sense of integrity and authenticity; neither of which are going to make you genuinely happy on a long-term basis. Being a people pleaser ultimately means you rank at the very bottom of your list of priorities, and that is beyond rubbish all round.

So, if you always consider what others will want and what will make *them* happy, it may be time to start thinking about *you*. For if you keep putting others' needs before your own, you will end up attracting real abusers, takers and needy people into your life, and you'll end up deeply resentful, depleted and empty. So, what can you do to turn things around? Here are some suggestions:

- Your self-worth is all down to you and how you perceive yourself, it's not dependant on approval from others. You don't need a huge thumb's up from others to be worthy on any level.
- Even if you're the kindest, nicest and most sparkly person in the whole world, you need to know not everyone is going to like you. You'll still naturally rub some people up the wrong way, but that's okay! You don't like everyone

you meet, do you? You can admit here, I won't tell anyone; promise! Worrying about those who do like you means you can give them the quality time and focus they deserve.

- Knowing the only person whose happiness you can control is your own. You can be a lovely person to make it easier for them to be happy, but that doesn't mean they *will* be. Each person is in charge of their own emotions.

- Realise most people are very wrapped up in their own lives. Most people won't take as much notice of all the people-pleasing things you do, or care as much as you may want them to. Being a people pleaser is ultimately the most colossal waste of time and energy.

- Try to be assertive. This may prove to be a real tricky one, especially as an awful lot of people avoid confrontation like the plague. But being assertive is not about aggression and dominance, it's about having healthy boundaries and learning to say no. If you are assertive with a loving heart, you will make your own needs be genuinely heard and respected. No is a full sentence and doesn't need justification or explanation.

- Practise self-care by ensuring every decision you make has your own needs at the heart of it. Rather than doing what you think is expected of you, or trying to please others, you need to see that you're important too.

- Love yourself and treat yourself in line with this. You are so awesome, and deserve respect and kindness. See yourself as your own special best friend, and treat yourself in this way always.

- Take an honest look at your own insecurities without judgement. By looking objectively at the underlying issues behind your people-pleasing behaviour, you'll be able to take steps to turn things around to a more positive outlook. This should be done without judging yourself for having these issues, for that will only add more problems to the table. Seek out a mental health professional to help you with this if you need to.

Fearing change

Whether it's your career, health, home life or relationships – dealing with any kind of change can seem really overwhelming. But when you hold extreme fear about change, you'll find you're invariably blocking yourself from moving forward and grabbing opportunities. Every new twist will come with a side dish of 'what if...?' coated with a sauce of negativity. You future project, but every daydream is based around the worst possible outcome – the failure, the losses and the disappointment. When you're deep in fear it's hard to see change as an exciting new opportunity for putting you where you need to be (as most change is). For, even if you hate your life and are bored of the monotony and tedious routine, at least there are no surprises. Life is safe, even if it's coloured in shades of boring beige. Change means that your life can suddenly move completely out your comfort zone, and you'll have no idea what may or may not happen. Better to be safe and miserable, right? I mean, at least you know what to expect every day. Wrong! Change is as natural a part of life as breathing is for us, and resisting it will just make life so much harder than it's meant to be. Every day we move through the changes of the sun rising and setting. Each year sees us move through the seasons, with all the aspects of death and rebirth they bring. Change is life, and be accepting it into your own life, you'll find that all areas start to flow easier for you. So, how can you flip your fear around?

1. Replace expectations with plans. Holding expectations can lead to real disappointment, regardless of whether they're negative or positive in nature. Fear-based thoughts of what might happen will only end up closing you off to the windows of opportunity that may be lying in wait for you, and you'll be unable to see all the good things that are there

for you to make the most of. By the same token, having really high expectations on some teetering pedestal may mean you find it hard to live up to them in reality. The best way to move from one place to another smoothly is to plan tangible and measured action steps you can work through one step at a time. By placing you in control of the process, in ways you can achieve what you set your mind to, you'll find the fear that once surrounded the changes will begin to naturally evaporate.

2. Consider and plan for all possibilities. The unknown brings fear. Although it may be hard to concoct solid plans for all eventualities, you can consider the 2 or 3 options that are most likely to happen and look at them from all angles so you feel more in control and better prepared.

3. Take a step back from your own mind. You are in control of your own thoughts; your mind is not in control of you! When you allow your fear-based thoughts to have free rein in regards to speculating all kinds of worst-case scenarios, you'll naturally build up more and more fear until you're a blubbering mess on the floor. Instead, take a mental step back and breathe. Witness the thoughts, but know you have the power to control the focus of your thinking. By consciously shifting the base of each thought from fear to seeing the potential positive, you will take your fear back from the fear and feel more in control of the changes you're going through.

4. Know you're stronger than you think and can cope with anything. Thinking of the worst-case scenario (without buying into it so much you believe it's the only outcome), and how you would deal with it, helps you to see that you can cope, no matter what happens next. It's not about being pessimistic and expecting the worst, it just helps you to see that you are so much more capable and stronger than you give yourself credit for. Believing in yourself helps the

changes to come in as they're supposed to.

5. Focus on the things you can control. Future projecting about the changes can mean you see the widest picture of how things will be, rather than seeing the small details that make up the image. You may not be able to deal with the change as a whole entity in one go, but you can break it down into bite-size chunks and deal with the smaller issues that are part of the bigger picture. Focus on what you can deal with, and stop focusing on what you can't.

Living in the past

Do you often find yourself reminiscing about past events with a real fondness for the 'good old days'? There's nothing wrong with looking over your shoulder at your memories, but there's a huge difference between thinking about the past and living there. The past is familiar, knowable and safe. Even if your past wasn't a bed of roses, you know it like the back of your hand. There are no surprises or sudden twists to make you feel overwhelmed. But if you are continuously talking and thinking about what happened in the past, all it's doing is robbing you of the chance of fulling embracing *right now*! It may be more pleasant to daydream about your childhood sweetheart than face the problems in your marriage, or get swept up in the memories of that great job you had rather than facing your current unemployed status, but your life is happening now moment by moment.

The past is like watching the same repeats of your favourite television show over and over again. I'm a huge *Friends* fan for example. For me, it's the best programme that has ever been aired on TV, and I can happily watch the reruns countless times, despite the fact I've seen each episode at least ten times previously. I know the plots, the jokes and all the lines word for word, but this knowledge is like a delicious in-joke for me. I giggle in advance, knowing the funny moments a mile before they come. But, and this is a big one, that doesn't mean I don't watch anything else on TV. I'm not so focused on this one programme that I refuse to even contemplate anything being shown right now. It's all about balance. If you're not careful, you could be so obsessed over what was, you miss the magic and joy of the now.

Living in the past can also be a by-product of fear towards your future. Yes, the future is full of possibility, but that also means it's full of uncertainty as well. Although we may have dreams, goals and wishes about every aspect of our future, we can't be entirely sure what *is* going to happen, and that can be really unnerving. And, scariest of all, what if our best days are behind us and our future is nothing but beige?

If thinking of your future leaves you feeling desperately anxious, and you're avoiding making long-term plans, this future fear may be a part of your thinking. Thinking of what could happen next may bring a plethora of frustration, and you may see yourself as being a real victim stuck where you are. Thankfully (mercifully), there are things you can do to help flip this around to a happier mindset:

- Get back to your gratitude groove by switching your focus to everything you have in your life to be thankful for.
- Try to make tangible and measured goals for future events. Having clear plans and action steps in your head will help to make the future a lot less scary.
- Breathe and accept you can't control everything. Look, I know this is going to be hard for some of you, but if you can get to grips with this unshakeable truth you will make your life run a hell of a lot smoother. There are always going to be areas of your life you can't do anything about. Situations where you'd do a lot better to go with the flow. Once you can get your head around this, you'll feel as though a huge weight has been taken off your shoulders.

There's a wonderful quote to keep in your head if living in the past is one of your issues. It's been attributed to a fair few people (seriously, just try Googling it!), but whoever said it first it definitely rings true:

Yesterday is history, tomorrow is a mystery, today is a gift; that's why they call it the present!

Putting yourself down

I'm a British woman, and as such know this one all too well. It seems to be part of our stereotypical charm to be self-deprecating and not blow our own trumpet, but I'm telling you this behaviour is not doing any of us any favours. We live in a world where there are hundreds of haters and cynical grump monkeys waiting to put us down. If you start joining in with the tidal wave of negativity against yourself, all you're doing is giving them a big thumb's up. Not only are your digs at yourself giving them permission to do the same thing, but you're also excusing the ones they've already thrown at you. Hardly waving the happy banner, is it?

Where does it come from? Well, maybe you've been the victim of bullying in the past, or maybe the receiver of a few offhanded comments that have smacked your self-esteem into the floor. Many of those who chuck jokes around like this are trying to make others like them by donning their witty cap, but when you're on the receiving end of such barbed comments it can seem the furthest thing away from funny. We are all aware that many jokes contain a grain of truth, and when you're already suffering from low confidence it can set you spinning into a downward spiral of pity. So, what do we do? The only answer seems to put on your suit of self-deprecating armour. If you can get the digs in about yourself before anyone else does, then it'll all be okay. But all this really does is put you in a position where you are being put down more than you have been in your entire life.

How can we flip things around then to start living a happier life? Imagine if you heard some of the terrible things you say about yourself every day aimed at someone you love – wouldn't you be angry and upset? (If the answer to this is a no, you may want to look at who you're spending your time with!) What makes you different? By belittling yourself repeatedly you are holding a big sign up to the world that you are irrelevant and unworthy. This is a dangerous place to put yourself in, for when you don't like yourself, you'll end up attracting people into yourself who are a mirror to this attitude. People who use you, abuse you and treat you really badly. Believe me, angel, you definitely deserve better than that. Here are three things you can start to bring into your life every time you feel yourself starting to put yourself down:

1. Bite your tongue. Not literally (it hurts a lot), but stop the words coming out of your mouth. Take a second to consider whether you would say these words to your family or friends. If the answer is a big fat 'NO', then catch the words before they have a chance to escape.

2. Think about how they may feel. Consider how your family, friends and colleagues feel to hear your self-deprecations on a daily basis. They may be trying to boost you up, and to hear you contesting that will be a painful process. Stand back from yourself and listen to the words you say. You'll start to understand how it's not benefitting anyone.

3. Replace each negative with a positive. If you can't stop the put-downs from coming, add a 'but I can do this...' or a 'but I am...' on the end of it. If you replace the word 'but' with 'and' you start to train your mind to focus on the positives rather than reaching for the put-downs every time. People (including yourself) believe something if they hear it often enough. Don't let anyone make you feel you're not worthy or a waste of oxygen. It's time to start spinning this situation 180 degrees so everyone can see the amazing qualities and attributes you do have!

Please, for the sake of your own self-worth and to help have healthy relationships with those around you, stop putting yourself down.

You matter. You are important. You deserve to be happy.

It's time you started to see that too.

Overthinking

Overthinking is a great stealer of happiness, pure and simple. I've lost track of the number of times I've turned situations round and round inside my head. You know it's becoming borderline obsessive when you find yourself unable to sleep because your brain won't shut up. Tell me it's not just me that has lain in bed, closed my eyes, and my brain has chosen that moment to go over everything that has ever happened in my whole life, as well as every possible future scenario that could possibly occur? Really, brain, really?

First of all, overthinking is akin to grabbing your brightest highlighter pen and swiping over the same problem relentlessly until the ends of time and space. Your mind only believes what you tell it, and if you keep focusing on what you believe is a problem in your life, you're simply telling your brain that it *is* a problem. The quagmire of crap will be up to your nose before you know it. Even scarier, consider this:

How many hours do you spend overthinking?

1 hour? 2? Think of the more productive and happier things you could be doing with that time and energy! Even an extra hour everyday could mean you could learn a new language, spend quality time with your friends and family, write that book you've been talking about for years, or do some exercise. The possibilities are endless, and yet we'd rather waste our precious moments building mountains out of molehills in our head. Which brings us to another point: overthinking puts the blocks on finding any real solutions to your problem. You get so caught up in the issue itself it becomes like the mental equivalent of picking at a scab on your skin. How's it going to get any better if you keep picking at the

same problem? Sometimes the best thing to do is leave it alone and give it the room it needs to breathe; the problem may soon just fix itself.

Your imagination is one of the most precious gifts your body possesses. The human mind has the incredible ability to visualise, create and imagine things more wonderful than anything seen on Heaven or Earth. Intergalactic worlds, magical creatures, and beings no human has ever seen with their physical eyes, and so much more – all imaginings the brain is able to create with just the slightest prompt to start the process. What a fantastic ability we all have! So, how do we choose to use this special gift? By worrying about future events and concocting situations that haven't happened, and may not happen at all. What a waste! When you free up your mind from overthinking, just think of the freedom your imagination will have to create magic and wonderment!

Finally, spending your time in overthinking mode stops you living in the here and now, so you're unable to be fully present in your life as it's happening. You start to doubt yourself and your natural intuitive leanings that would allow you to successfully solve the issue; the noise of your overworked mind becomes too loud. How are you supposed to link in to your happiness when you're focused on indecision, anxiety, confusion and fear? Basically, in one complete crappy nutshell – overthinking will squash your chances for being happy harder than a blue whale dropping on an egg (that'd be weird though...). So, how can we flip things around to stop the monster before it gets out of hand?

There are a number of things you can utilise to put you back in control. Firstly, ask yourself if this issue will matter a year down the line, or even in a month. So many of us allow minor things in our lives to have far too much of our attention and energy. By putting the issue into a wider perspective, you are better able to see it for what it is, and choose to use your time on things that are more important in your life. Another effective trick is to give yourself a time limit on making the decision you need to make in order to help you out of the problem. Doing this provides you an exit door away from the overthinking box, and places you back in the driving seat of your own life. For example, for minor decisions like whether I should put the bins out now or do it later, I allow myself no longer than 30 seconds to come to a definite decision. For bigger life decisions, I try to set myself no longer than 30 minutes. Notice how I say 'try' in that sentence. This tip doesn't always work, because some events in your life are so complex or tragic, it can be hard to remove emotion out of the way. Like anything in your life though, the more you practise, the easier it becomes. Giving yourself the intention of a set time limit means you're less likely to turn things over for hours, days, or even weeks.

Another good tip is to understand that you can't control every tiny detail of your life. Overthinking does allow you to examine every possibility so you can try to ensure that you won't make any mistakes or risk any kind of failure. But life doesn't work like that! Making mistakes and going through failures are valuable lessons that help us to grow. Countless celebrities who you may admire and look up to have experienced failure in their own life:

- Walt Disney – Today, the global mammoth that is Disney makes billions of dollars from merchandise, movies and theme parks around the world, but Walt Disney himself didn't have the most successful of career starts. He was fired by a newspaper editor because: 'he lacked imagination and had no good ideas.' After that, Disney started several businesses that didn't last too long and ended with bankruptcy and failure. He kept going, however, and eventually found the keys to success that worked.
- Bill Gates – Gates didn't seem to be the type who would become one of the most successful men in the world after he dropped out of Harvard and started a failed first business with Microsoft co-founder Paul Allen, called Traf-O-Data. While this early idea didn't work, Gates' later work did,

creating the global empire that is Microsoft.

- Fred Astaire – In his first screen test, the testing director of MGM noted that Astaire, *'Can't act. Can't sing. Slightly bald. Can dance a little.'* Astaire went on to become an incredibly successful actor, singer and dancer and kept that note in his Beverly Hills home to remind him of his beginnings.

- Stephen King – The first book by this author, the iconic thriller *Carrie*, received 30 rejections, finally causing King to give up and throw it in the trash. His wife fished it out and encouraged him to resubmit it, and the rest is history, with King now having hundreds of books published, and the distinction of being one of the best-selling authors of all time.

- Oprah Winfrey – Most people know Oprah as one of the most iconic faces on TV as well as one of the richest and most successful women in the world. Oprah faced a hard road to get to that position, however, enduring a rough and often abusive childhood as well as numerous career setbacks including being fired from her job as a television reporter because she was *'unfit for TV.'*

- JK Rowling – When Rowling wrote the first *Harry Potter* book, she was divorced, bankrupt and on benefits. After a dozen publishers rejected her manuscript one finally agreed to publish it. But the publisher told Rowling that she needed to get a job because there's no money in children's books. She's now a billionaire.

Failures may look incredibly negative and devastating at first, but there's so much to gain from them. They help you to grow, and give you invaluable knowledge of what will work and what won't work for your future endeavours. You can't control everything in life, there are too many variables and other people to take into consideration. Yes, it's easier said than done, but if you start with minor things in your life you can build up to the big stuff. Start by letting someone else clean the house, or cook the dinner. You may be itching to jump in and take over, but if you can let someone else run the show with the smaller things, you'll see how the world doesn't fall apart if you're not always in charge. And the fact that if things do go wrong, life still goes on.

The other way to calm the chattering monkey mind of overthinking is through engaging in a gentle conversation with it, in which you are able to challenge the fears it keeps presenting to you. For example:

Monkey mind: *If you lose your job, you'll have no money!*
Me: *Okay, and what's the worst thing that could happen?*
Monkey mind: *You won't be able to pay the rent and you'll lose your home!*
Me: *Will anybody die if that happens?*
Monkey mind: *Erm... no. I guess not.*
Me: *Well, it's just a house. We can always find somewhere else to live, can't we?*
Monkey mind: *Yeah, suppose so.*
Me: *Okay, so can we cope if we do lose the house?*
Monkey mind: *Yes, we can cope.*

Ta-da! One calm monkey mind! To be honest, it doesn't always work, but it does sometimes. It's certainly worth taking the time to have a chat with the screeching monkey inside your brain and establishing just what is going on and if it's worthwhile really panicking or not. The good thing about the fear monkey is, most of the time, the fear inside your head isn't actually as bad in reality as it would let you believe. The fear monkey is a real pro at blowing things out of all proportion, and seeing terrifying things on every corner. When you point out that things aren't that bad, it breathes out all of that stress and anxiety, and then you can get on with your life.

Finally, consciously spending more time in the present moment is an effective way of flipping the overthinking habit to a more positive place. You can do this by deliberately slowing any task you're working on. Let's have a little practice so you can see what I mean. I'm a quick reader, always have been, and my eyes zoom through each line of text as if they're in the Olympic 100 metre race against Usain Bolt. Instead:

Let's **(pause)**
read **(pause)**
each **(pause)**
line **(pause)**
slower.

When you make the effort to slow everything down, you become much more aware of your body and what's happening around you in this present moment. If the overthinking habit starts to sneak in (and it will, it's a cheeky little monkey), shout, **'STOP!'** in your mind or even out loud if you have to (though you may get some odd looks from those around you!). Disrupting the thoughts then gives you the space to reconnect with the present moment you're experiencing right now. Taking it all in with all five of your senses quietens the mind down, and brings you back to the present.

All of the things listed above originate from the ego. This is a natural part of your being, but can be a tricky little monkey to deal with. Ultimately, there are two kinds of ego: the negative and the positive. The positive ego centres on our sense of self: who we are, our history and our place in the world. It is through the ego that we make sense of the world around us, as well as ourselves. Without it, you'd be lost in a world more confusing than *Alice in Wonderland*. In contrast, the negative ego is the part of us that is totally centred on fear. There are two kinds of fear in life: fear that is good and fear that is most definitely bad.

The good type of fear can be found when there's an immediate threat to your physical survival, and it allows you to deal with this in the short term. It makes your heart beat that bit faster. It makes you cross the street when you sense there's something slightly off about the person in front of you. This fear gives you sudden strength on a superhero scale that allows you to deal with things that are proving immediately hazardous to your health, or those you care about. Good fear is all about protection of ourselves and the people we love. And, although it's deeply rooted in our psyche as an innate part of our being, it is something we only want to use a couple of times throughout our life, if at all.

But not all fear behaves in this way. Bad fear has exactly the same symptoms as the good kind – your heart begins to race; your palms are sweaty and your whole body feels on edge – but it's the origin of that fear that is truly the sticking point. Fear that is bad for us is negative because it's deeply rooted in one question:

WHAT IF?
What if I get sick?
What if we lose all our money?
What if they don't like me?
What if I fail?
What if I never meet my one true love?

Fear in the short term can be a good thing as it keeps us safe and alert to real dangers, but fear in the long term does nothing but seek to wear us down. Trapped in a web of mediocrity, we curse the world for making us so scared, but are too afraid to change our lives for the better! For those out there who worry about taking the leap of faith and chasing their dreams, the pay-off is to stay stuck where they don't want to be. Afraid of going after their desired career but hating their current job; afraid of being on their own, but miserable in the relationship they're in; scared of moving to a better life but worn down by the greyness of their existence. Yes, change can be disconcerting, but fear does nothing but keep you stuck in misery. And you deserve so much better! You deserve a life of excitement, passion and happiness, none of which have anything to do with fear. So, if we know this, why are we allowing ourselves to be stuck in the depths of fear?

It's worth noting here that I'm not saying we should get rid of fear altogether; that would be practically impossible. Fear is an innate and natural part of our being. Fear keeps us safe and alerts us to possible dangers and life-threatening situations so we can protect ourselves. Neither can you get rid of the ego part of the self. After all, we know that what you resist persists and all things have purpose, so why put so much force and resistance against the actions and feelings that come forth as a result of our ego? Repressing something never completely makes it go away but actually suppresses and hides the real core of the reason it manifested in the first place. Eventually, what has been repressed will surface again to make its truth known. This is the exact case with the ego and may be the reason so many in the world that have worked from these teachings have had trouble moving to a new, more permanent, state of mind and being. It also may be the main reason their ego keeps creating what they don't want while simultaneously keeping them from what they truly desire.

The negative ego in essence is an innate tool within our heads that, if left unchecked, can go rogue on our ass. Sometimes the best thing you can do is have a word or two with it:

Dear Ego,

Look, I know you want to keep me safe. I know you're terrified of the 'what ifs' and you can't help but focus on the worst-case scenario. I get it; that's you. That's your thing. But, listen – you're doing my head in. I'm tired of listening to your whining and moaning; it's boring. So, why don't you do us both a favour and shut the hell up for a while, yeah? I've got big work to do, and you're giving me a headache. Don't worry, I've got this! I know where I'm going and I know what I'm doing. Just sit back, and I don't know... do some

colouring or something.
Lots of love (you need it)
Me xx

Working through the tips and exercises included here will help remove things from your life that are robbing you of your happiness. Like everything, these things will take time and practice to be effective, so don't be hard on yourself if it doesn't come naturally to you. You're human and are doing the best you can. This book is to help you be happier in your life overall, so let's not pull ourselves down into judgements and nastiness. It's a process, but one that can sprinkle magic over your whole life!

You are better
than unicorns,
rainbows
and sparkles
combined. And
that is pretty
amazing!

Things I will always be open to:

- A trip to a bookshop or library
- Snuggly fuzzy socks (especially rainbow ones)
- Chocolate. Anytime, any place.
- Cuddles
- Talking to and petting animals
- Massages
- Coffee mugs as big as your head
- Chats with friends that are full of real soul baring and cheeky giggles!
- Retro references from my childhood (hello 80s and 90s)
- Anything that's covered in glitter or rainbows... or both!

Unicorns Believe in You

When you were younger did you believe in Santa, the Easter Bunny and the Tooth Fairy? Chances are you did; most kids believe in them from anywhere to the ages of 6 to 10. It's an accepted part of childhood that we all pass down and accept with joyful glee. So, let's say you believed in these magical beings for around 8 years of your life without any serious question, why is it then that you find it so hard to believe in yourself for 5 minutes?

Mind blown, right?

When I first heard this idea, my jaw hit the floor. We find it so easy to believe in others more than ourselves, that we'll extend this to beings that there is not one iota of tangible proof for. When you think about that, it all seems beyond crazy, doesn't it?

(If you still believe in the aforementioned beings of wonderment by the by, I'm not here to burst your bubble. You're perfectly entitled to believe in whatever you please, so you carry on spreading the magic. Sparkly high fives all round!)

I need to tell you what not believing in yourself achieves... nothing!

Nothing, nada, zip, zilch, zero!

You've got more chance of making your dreams come true by rubbing every lamp down the car boot sale on a Sunday than trying to make it all happen but not believing in yourself. Sure, amazing stuff may just happen to fall magically into your lap regardless of whether you believe in yourself or not; sometimes life works that way. But the chances are you're going to end up in a place that does nothing but make you miserable, frustrated and feeling like a total victim. Hardly sounds like an exciting place to be, does it?

The biggest difference between successful people and unsuccessful people isn't intelligence or opportunity or resources. It's the belief that they can make their goals happen. It doesn't matter how many skills, qualifications or friends in high places you have – if you don't believe in your ability to be happy and successful, it won't happen! Well... it might happen, but it's going to be a hell of a lot harder to transform the cards you've been dealt into something real and tangible. A bit like trying to saw through a plank of wood with a spoon; why make life unnecessarily hard on yourself?

It's easy to ponder on why so many of us find it difficult to believe in ourselves. After all, we seem to be bombarded with messages telling us how vital it is at every turn, from the Cheryl hair flick of L'Oréal (*'You're worth it'*), to the sport driven beat of Nike (*'Just do it'*). Never have we been so saturated by so many slogans, messages and campaigns as we are right now, and yet never has worth been so measured by the end result. If you succeed and accomplish something that others deem good, then you are worthy; then you are good enough. But what if you don't climb that proverbial mountain? What if you don't find a cure for cancer/invent the latest must-have gadget/release a number one album? Does that make you somehow less worthy than those who do? And who gets to make those decisions anyway?

See, I have this belief. Some may call it downright crazy and look at me as though I've just gone shopping in my pants and socks (**scary thought!**), but I believe it to be 100% true. Here it is. You may want to brace yourself for the inevitable shock that's sure to follow:

You are worthy because you are here. You matter because you are alive.

Okay, yes, if you can achieve great things in your lifetime, that's incredible. No one is taking away from those amazing achievements in the slightest. All I *am* saying is that if you don't manage to achieve big things during your life, then that doesn't make you any less than anyone else. Goodness knows there's enough pressure and expectation from everywhere else; bucket loads of it! If it's not the media, it's your family, your friends, your partner, your boss. Everywhere you look people are measuring themselves and you by some constructed league table that doesn't really exist. Don't start judging yourself too, you deserve better than to play that game.

Besides anything else, if you don't believe in yourself, who will? If you are unable to believe in your ability and worth to succeed in whatever it is you set your heart on, then you're going to have a difficult time expecting anyone else to believe in you too! You'll just end up surrounded by people who see you as worthless, disappointing and not capable of anything; a complete mirror to your own beliefs. And you won't mind too much if they don't treat you well, because you wouldn't expect anything more. The minute you start to shift to self-belief, the whole game changes too. You won't put up with anyone who doesn't support you, and if they express views like that to you, they'll be kicked to the kerb faster than a wheelie bin on bin day!

And, if you can't stir up any kind of belief in the amazing person you are, you are going to make your journey so hard. The first time an obstacle comes your way you'll break like a twig and give up on yourself. The path to success is not a smooth one normally. There'll be challenges, setbacks and blockages on the way, and if you're not careful they'll stop you in your tracks. Having the kind of belief in yourself that you deserve to have means you'll end up with an unshakeable confidence in your own abilities that no number of obstacles can break. You'll believe so deeply in yourself and your dreams, that you'll see it as something to get over, rather than something to stop you.

It's worth noting here that self-belief doesn't necessarily equal success. It definitely makes the chances of success higher than if you didn't believe in yourself at all, but life doesn't come with guarantees. We are all likely to experience failure at some point, and it's also normal to allow this experience to knock your self-belief... temporarily. If you do fall off the horse, you got to get back on as quickly as possible, or you'll lose your nerve. Failing at something doesn't make you a failure overall, it means you're one step closer to where you need to be. Don't let the knock rob you of the belief you have in yourself, for nothing should take away something so precious. See it for what is: a learning experience and part of the journey, and then move forward from it.

Right now, you may be sitting thinking, 'This is all well and good, Katie. I get why I need to believe in myself, but how do I do it?' Countless coaches, writers and speakers talk about believing in yourself, but without the tools to do it you'll be in exactly the same position as you are now, and that's not worth anything to anyone. So, I'm going to share with you my secret, and it may prove to be just as jarring as the last one I shared, for it certainly goes against the grain of probably everything you've ever been taught about self-belief:

Believing in yourself doesn't start with you!

I know! Shocking, right? Surely that goes against everything I've spoken about so far, but I disagree. See, asking someone whose mind is clouded with doubts and fears to suddenly start believing in themselves is akin to asking the playground bully to give you all the love you've been searching for. Your own mind will obviously come into the process, but it can't be your first port of call, for initially you may seriously be lacking the love, acceptance and confidence you need to start the self-belief train moving along the track. Instead, consider the possibility of finding someone you can really trust who believes in you. They can act as your loving mirror, if they are happy to do so, and provide you with love, cheerleading and belief as you need it. As well as a loving kick up the bum from time to time! This may not be the easiest position to fill in your life, and you may find you have to find more than one as you both change and grow, but they are worth their weight in gold. By having someone who continually believes in you, you will start to grow belief in yourself.

Alongside this, consider showing your appreciation and belief for others. Think of at least ten people who have made a real difference in your life. This can be family, friends, teachers, or even celebrities; in this age of social media it's relatively easy to seek out the contact details of people. Send each of them a message that says:

> *I wanted you to know that you've been so important to my life. I was thinking about you today, and I just wanted to thank you for making a difference in my life. You are an amazing person.*

You don't have to do this to get anything back, but the more you can believe in others and allow others to believe in you, the more you can start to believe in yourself. Give yourself that gift, for it will make your soul smile brighter than the sun.

Why be moody
when you can
shake your
booty?

The Time is Now

Are you one of those people who is continually waiting for some magical future before they can be happy? You know the ones I mean:

When I'm thin, then I'll be happy.
If I won the Lottery, it would fix everything.
When I meet the love of my life, then I can finally be happy.

Why are you waiting to be happy?
What if, horror of horrors, you could be happy *right now*?
I know! Scary, right?
How many films or TV shows have you watched over the years that feature some geeky individual that fashion forgot (normally a woman)? They are the person who is ignored, teased or flat out bullied, and they certainly aren't getting the love of their life anytime this century. Then, a miracle occurs. The sad little individual is given a life-changing makeover, which leaves them hotter than the Sahara Desert in the middle of summer. Suddenly everyone wants to be their friend, they land their dream job, and their crush damn near trips over their own tongue at the hottie in front of them. Happy ending, right? The moral of the story clearly being that no one, not even life itself, is going to be loving you looking like that, honey! You better get a team of stylists over stat before you even raise any eyebrow, let alone anything more substantial!
Seriously?!?
What a load of utter crap! It's no wonder so many people struggle with the idea of loving themselves, we're hardly given inspirational stories in this field to aspire to. Add to this the fact we are constantly bombarded with magazines and advertisements that make us feel as though we need to improve ourselves as soon

as possible, and most of us aren't giving ourselves the kind of love that we really need:

Get a flat tummy in 7 days!
Sexier Cleavage: How to Get a Rise Out of Your Man
Hungry Girls' Guide to Losing Weight
The New Skinny Pills: Yes, They Work!
Get an Insane Body. It's Hard, But You'll Look Hot!
Drop a Dress Size by Tonight!
What Guys Hate for You to Wear in Bed

Hardly inspiring and confidence boosting stuff, hey? We're all inundated with messages like this every single day; hundreds of them all telling us we're not good enough. It's kind of hard to love and accept yourself as you are when you're constantly told that you shouldn't. Give me your hand for a second… you are amazing just the way you are. I want you to believe that, because it's the truest truth I can give to you. Let me explain why it's so important that you give yourself some much-needed love, starting right this very second.

First of all, it may be the done thing to be a self-deprecating, blushing wallflower who bats every compliment away harder than a Wimbledon champion, but hating on yourself is not going to help you be a better person any time soon. Every single one of us has things about themselves that they don't like. Every person has parts of themselves that they know could do with a little improving, for we're human and fallible ones at it. The problem comes when these imperfections become your entire focus, and you throw nothing at yourself but self-loathing and never-ending criticism. If your house was falling into disrepair, you wouldn't approach it with constant disdain in the hope it would have the motivation to fix itself as if by magic. No, you'd give the place some loving TLC. Give anything in your life nothing but your hatred and anger, and it's not going to respond well, and this is certainly the case for people. Giving yourself love, care and time doesn't mean you're being indulgent or selfish, it means you have the strength you need to improve and do better.

Besides, no one, and I mean NO ONE is perfect. No, not even the supermodels, actors or singers you see in every gossip magazine. These glamorous celebrities may look as though they have all the answers and are the happiest people in the world, but appearances can be deceptive. Imagine hearing someone say, *'I tell you, I'm perfect. There's nothing about me that can be improved.'* What would you think of them? That they were either totally delusional, or had an ego bigger than Jupiter, right? If you can see that there are parts of yourself that need improving, that doesn't make you weak or a terrible person – it means you're amazing! You have the strength to have honest self-reflection, and you have the determination to be more and do more than who you right now. Not only that, but you're motivated enough to try and do better. You're not weak, terrible or lazy – far from it! You know that your future self is a fabulous and inspirational rock star, and you're going to do what it takes to make this vision a reality. And let me tell you something else as well: all the qualities you want to manifest, all the amazing attributes you want to have, are all within you already. All you need is a bit of love and nurturing and they're yours!

Our culture values finding love above nearly everything else. Countless songs, stories, films and advertising all seem to be geared towards this topic, as though nothing else could ever be as seemingly important as this life's goal. I'm not saying that looking for someone to love you isn't a good thing, by the by. When you have people around you that can comfort, encourage and support you, it truly is one of the best feelings in the world. The problems arise, however, when we're led to believe that you can only get this kind of love and acceptance from other people. Self-love is just as valid and important as the love you can receive from others; more so in fact. I know you've read that with a raised eyebrow, but let me explain.

When you love yourself, it's like wearing an invisible crown on your head 24/7. This isn't to stop you doing what you need to do anyway, but focuses you as the Queen/King you are. Loving yourself to this extent *right now* means your standards will rise up to meet your new fabulous level. When you're hating on yourself, you may not recognise when others don't treat you with the love and respect you deserve, or worse still, you'll see or think it's acceptable. Why should you deserve better when your opinion of yourself is on the floor? Ultimately, we attract people into our lives who reflect how we feel about ourselves. Think you're a waste of space who is ugly, fat and not going to achieve much in life? Hey, guess what? Your relationships (and this is *all* relationships, not just the kissy-face type) aren't going to be the healthiest in the world either. You'll end up with friends, partners, work colleagues, and even family members who treat you like pants. And, let me ask you, how are these bad relationships going to impact on your already fledgling self-esteem? Yep, that's right, they're going to send you hurtling down a one-way spiral to the floor. Pity party for one – shall I bring a bottle?

Let's say you do end up in a relationship that is of the healthy and happy nature, but you're still struggling with the whole loving yourself thing. In all relationships, you have to be a good example of how you want the other person to treat you. Yes, you're two individual people who are both responsible for communication, compassion and understanding, but your example counts for more than you could ever realise. Let's say you're trying a healthy eating plan and you have a big carb-fest blowout. You immediately start beating yourself up and feeling as though you're a failure. Your partner witnesses this, and ends up thinking you're the type who needs a big dose of tough love to motivate you, when what you really need is telling how proud they are of the hard work you've done so far; that this blowout is not the end of the world and you should put it behind you; and questioning how they can support you to make better choices next time. Basically, to give you so much support that you can see how truly super-duper amazing you really are! If you've never learned how to love yourself, or even understand that this is something you deserve to have, it's going to be harder for those around you to know what love you want and deserve.

Oh, and by the way, social media doesn't help either. Now, don't get me wrong – I freaking **love** social media! Facebook and Instagram are my favourites, and you'll happily find me posting and hash-tagging the day away on a regular basis. *But...* your lives are now exposed to a bigger audience than ever before. We paint every aspect of our lives on the big screen of the World Wide Web for everyone to see, and you never know who may be looking. Millions of people, all with their own opinions, preferences and beliefs. Get thousands of likes and shares, and you're beaming all the way up to cloud 9. But find yourself at the mercy of arguments, haters, or even trolls, and it can feel as though your whole world can come crashing down. Over a long period of time of being exposed to this kind of negativity, your self-esteem can be totally broken down, and it's complete and utter horse poop. The only opinions that you should really take to heart are from those who genuinely know you, love you, and understand the kind of person you are. For those who don't come to the table with this same level of love for you, that doesn't mean you need to ignore them. Actually, talking to people whose opinion differs from yours can be hugely beneficial on both sides, and lead to an expansion of understanding of the world. But, you should never allow anyone to make you hate yourself **ever**! It's a good idea to have the self-reflection to consider whether what you're posting is totally uncalled for and nasty, but you can do it whilst still having an unconditional bubble of love placed all the way around you; unbreakable and everlasting. Never let anyone or anything pierce your perfect bubble of love, no matter how many followers they may have.

So, now we know why self-love is so vital for you, do you really want to wait to bring these blessings into your life? Do you want to live with bucket loads of negativity, fear and hatred until you get to some magical point in the future? What if, just maybe, you never actually make this dream come true? You don't win the lottery, meet the love of your life, or lose all the weight – are you still going to be hating on yourself? If you've just answered *'Yes'* to that question by the way, put this book down right now and focus on your self-esteem issues. No amount of explaining how to be happy is going to make even the smallest dent in how you feel about yourself until you address the underlying issues. I give you the biggest hug I can send you, and I urge you to get the help you need. No one deserves to feel that badly about themselves, not even you.

How can you start to love yourself now? There are a number of things that you can do, as well as things that you would be advised to avoid. The good stuff first:

- Be kind to yourself, always.
- When you look in the mirror, focus on the parts of yourself you like and smile.
- Accept compliments with a 'Thank you' rather than automatically batting them away.
- When others give you praise, allow the glow over it to sit with you for a while. Focus on how good it makes you feel all the way to your core, and don't immediately run to a criticism of yourself as you would normally.
- If you make mistakes, don't verbally and mentally tear chunks out of yourself. Everyone makes mistakes, it's part of life. It doesn't make you a bad person. Give yourself love and understanding instead.
- Know your worth (remember that invisible crown!), and stand up for yourself when you need to. Being assertive is a good thing, it doesn't mean you need to be aggressive or violent in any way.

- Treat yourself as though you are your best friend every single day.
- Your individuality and uniqueness should be celebrated, no matter how quirky that may be. In fact, the quirkier the better!
- Be your authentic self in every moment without excuse, and don't let your worry about what others may think of you cloud this focus.
- Speak your truth, even if your voice shakes.

Whilst this list is clearly focused on how you can start to be more loving to yourself, the things for you to avoid is centred on the removal of judgements towards the self. The more you can shift away from these kind of negative self-judgements, the more you can allow the self-love pour into your heart. These are:

- Stop hating on yourself for every tiny little thing. Notice the ticker tape of hate that feeds through your brain *all the time*... isn't it so exhausting, not to mention boring? Noticing it is the first step to changing it, so don't dismiss this bit. Oh, and don't criticise yourself for having these judgements about yourself; that does nothing but bring more unnecessary crappage (crap-filled baggage) to the table.
- Don't bat away every compliment as though you're trying out for a baseball team. The people who give you them may stop if you repeatedly do this, you know.
- Don't belittle yourself or put yourself down, even if you do it with humour. Your mind only believes what you keep telling it, and these comments will eventually become your truth.
- When talking to someone, don't let your faults lead the way. Imagine if you're talking to someone and they do nothing but put themselves down. Hardly someone you

want to keep talking to! Ditch the self-deprecation in the deepest, darkest pit ASAP.

- Listen up, this bit is super important: if someone hurts you, it's not okay! Rationalising it away with excuses, and justifying their behaviour, is madness. No one deserves to treat you in this way, no matter how much they try to blame you. It's not your fault and it's not okay.

- If someone says they love you, that's one of the most beautiful gifts you can give to another human. So, if that same person starts treating you with indifference and as though you're some kind of afterthought, that's hardly up there with love-filled behaviour. Loving someone means treating them with respect, empathy and kindness. Any kind of indifference towards you is *not* love.

- Be careful of broadcasting the fact you have low self-esteem. Not everyone has the same morals and integrity as you do, and there are people out there who will take advantage of what you've shared with them. Crappy I know, but it can happen. Take it from someone who knows, you don't want to head down this path. If you need to talk to someone about it, make sure it's someone you completely trust, and who you know will love and support you. Anything less isn't worth a second of your precious time.

- There will be times in your life when you come across people who are in a really bad place, and will use you to express these issues. Their behaviour will thus show itself as greed, selfishness, fear, hatred and anger. Let me make something crystal clear, just in case you've missed the point I've been trying to hammer home to you: it's not okay for someone to treat you badly. Don't accept excuses, or someone trying to make out as though it's your fault. Yes, it's super scary, but sometimes you need to speak up. Sometimes you need to stand up for yourself and let them know that you won't tolerate their bad behaviour. Your future self will thank you for your courage.

Deciding to love and accept yourself right now is a big deal that cannot be underestimated. The power of this decision causes ripples to circle throughout your life, and will leave its lasting impression on every corner. Ultimately, it will help you realise that you don't have to wait to be happy. You can be happy right now if you choose to be. Hell, you deserve to be happy right now! Stop putting your happiness off as though it's not important, as though you don't deserve to be happy. You do deserve it in spades; it's your undeniable right as the fabulous person you are! Focus on what will literally turn that frown upside down and go and get it – what are you waiting for?

As a side note, if this is something you're hugely struggling with, there are two things that you can do to help your mind to accept the idea. First of all, write a letter from your ten-year-old self to you now. Imagine what your child self wants to hear. Who do they need you to be? What do they hope you've achieved? The second task is then to write a letter to yourself from you ten years from now. What does your future self want you to know right now? What would they like you to do more of, and what do you need to stop doing? Considering these two valuable letters will help you see that putting your happiness off to some future time is robbing you of living your life right now. I guarantee that both your 10-year-old self and your future self both want you to start putting your happiness first and living the life you deserve to have. You owe it to them and you to start right now!

You are
awesome.
Unicorns are
awesome.
Therefore,
you must be a
unicorn!

The Ultimate Happy Playlist

Music is magical. No matter what mood I'm in, all I need to do is stick on my favourite uplifting songs and I'm soon bouncing happily along again. I feel we all need some happy songs in our life. Listening to moving music causes the brain to release dopamine, a feel-good chemical. People love music for much the same reason they're drawn to sex, drugs, gambling and delicious food – because it makes them feel deliciously good! You may have your own positive tunes to put the spring back in your step, but these are mine:

- Sax by Fleur East
- Can't Stop the Feeling by Justin Timberlake
- Uptown Funk by Mark Ronson and Bruno Mars
- Happy by Pharrell Williams
- You've Got the Love by The Source featuring Candi Staton
- Don't Stop Me Now by Queen
- Firework by Katy Perry
- I Wish by Stevie Wonder
- Mr Blue Sky by ELO
- All Night Long by Lionel Richie
- Don't Be So Hard on Yourself by Jess Glynne
- Wings by Little Mix
- Shine by Take That
- Free by Estelle

Smile! Happiness looks simply beautiful on you.

Use Your Kindness Blaster 3000

One of the most negative phenomena of our times is the lorry load of stress that is dumped on our heads every day. I'm sure you're nodding your head with a wry smile; stress is something we are all far too familiar with. And, like me, you've probably tried a smorgasbord of ways to try and cope with the stress, right?

Alcohol = potential messy. Alcohol tends to increase the mood you were in before you started drinking. So having a few scoops when you're in a bad place rarely leads to a happy outcome. Besides, I don't know about you, but hangovers are definitely getting worse as I get older...

Overindulge in food = definitely not good for the waistline this one – especially when your go-to food is a sugar-laden, calorific party of one. Why is it that all the stuff that's really bad for you tastes *so* good?

Binge watching TV = see now, this starts off as being quite good. Maybe you've been meaning to catch up with the shows you've missed for ages, and you're quite excited to bring down the percentage on your overloaded digital planner. But when you've been mindlessly staring at the box for hours, you don't know what day it is, and you feel as though you and the sofa are becoming one, it may be time to try a different coping method.

Anything else? Well, we can also include:

- Spending too much money on stuff we don't need, and making our bank balance cry.
- Pushing yourself too hard with the exercise regime (angry exercising tends to mean going too far for too long, and major ouchies the next day).
- Ending up in romantic/sexy situations that you wouldn't touch with a barge pole if you weren't in a stressed-out mood (but that's for another book).

So, basically, we can see that the way we (read that *I*) have been trying to cope with stress is as much use as a fart in a spacesuit. Thank the angels above then that there is another way, and this way is pretty much guaranteed to make you and others smile from ear to ear. What is it?

Happiness!

When you do something kind for someone else, the levels of serotonin increase in the brain. This natural chemical is one of the key activators of making you feel happy, so it's certainly a good one to increase within your mind! Not only does it increase your levels, but the person on the receiving end of your kindness also receives a boost in their serotonin. So the more acts of kindness you do for others every day, the more you can help to keep yourself at a consistent happy level; and sparkle happiness out to others in the process!

When stress threatens to strike, blast it into smithereens with your Kindness Blaster. Doing so helps to shift your thinking and the mood you're in, and can give others the same amazing gift in the process. What acts of kindness can you do throughout your day?

- Stick up Post-it notes on every available space in your workplace or school with positive messages on them, such as 'you're beautiful', or 'you make a difference'.
- Offer to babysit for someone who can't normally afford to pay for anyone. To give overworked and stressed-out parents the wonderful gift of a night out will definitely put smiles on their faces.
- Pay the parking fee for the car behind you in the queue.
- When you've finished a really good book, why not leave it on a bus or train for someone else to read? You could even add a note inside suggesting that they could leave it for someone else to read once they've finished it.
- Offer cold glasses of water to the people delivering the mail

and parcels on a hot day.

- If you see someone's parking meter is about to expire, put some more change in it to give them extra time without getting a ticket.
- If you have coupons you're not going to use, take them with you to the shop and leave them next to the relevant product for someone else to find and use.
- When you're in a queue in a coffee shop, post office or supermarket, let someone else cut in front of you.
- Tweet or Facebook message a genuine compliment to three people right now.
- While you're out, compliment a parent on how well-behaved their child is.
- Smile at someone on the street, just because.
- Try to make sure every person in a group conversation feels included.
- Give someone a tissue who's crying in public, and offer to talk about it, but only if they want to.
- Help your elderly neighbour take out their bins or cut their grass.
- Keep an extra umbrella at work and let someone borrow it on their way home if there's a sudden downpour.

Please use your golden Kindness Blaster 3000 today. I can't promise that it'll zap all the stress away, but it'll certainly make you feel a whole lot better than you did, as well as feeling much more in control of your emotions. And, by blasting away your stress with kindness, you can also blast love into someone else's life; definitely a reason to smile!

Because when you stop and look around, life is pretty amazing.

The Comfort Zone

I feel as though this chapter should come with spooky background music:

You are now entering... The Comfort Zone!
(dum, dum, dum, duuum!)

Mind you, most of us are pretty comfortable and cosy in this zone; at least cosy enough to stay in the familiar routine it gives us. Even if that place gives us more greyness and flatness than a slug with the blues, at least we know what we're dealing with. Better that than the scary unknown with all of its endless possibility and chances for things to go wrong, right?

Did you ever see the film *Groundhog Day* with Bill Murray? It centres on a character called Phil Connors, a TV weatherman who finds himself having to cover the annual Groundhog Day event. However, he finds himself in a time loop, where he has to repeat the same day over and over again. Initially, this revelation leads to a certain amount of hedonism on his part, but the novelty soon wears off. The agony of living the same day on repeat is so traumatising that he considers taking his own life (I know this is a book on happiness, but don't worry; I'm making a point). The film climaxes with Connors re-examining his life and realising what's truly important, so that he can make the changes he needs to.

Why am I mentioning this? Well, my beautiful friend, the film makes a comment on the very thing we've been looking at. Did you ever feel as though your comfort zone had become so monotonous that you were on some giant hamster wheel, or maybe a never-ending treadmill? Life seems to go on and on, repeating the same thing over and over again. Hardly a situation that fills you full of joy. Don't get me wrong, for some the comfort zone can be a happy place. They like the routine, the safety and the familiarity of it all, but for most of us it doesn't exactly inspire great happiness.

To get something you've never had, you have to do something you've never done.
Unknown

Happiness arises from pushing ourselves, learning something new, feeling ourselves grow and develop, and going out of our way to help others. As scary as it may be, if you change just one thing – one tiny thing – you can help yourself to be happier in the long run. I'm not saying you need to go and do a naked bungee jump over a river of crocodiles (unless you want to, of course), but I just wanted you to consider a question: when did you last make a conscious decision to step a toe out of the comfort zone? What's the worst that could happen? If you don't like it or it's not what you thought it would be, then things will be able to go back to the way they were before.

Having the courage to take that step will give you so much: you can test your limits; feel as though all of your senses have been turned up to maximum; and gain a real sense of achievement. Your confidence will go through the roof, and this can then inspire you to go on to even bigger and better things. You have the power to set your life on fire! To experience truly dazzling emotions and a huge glitter bomb of excitement. Stepping out of your comfort zone will make you feel alive!

So, why do people stop themselves from doing it? Why aren't we all kicking our comfort zones in the bin? One word:

FEAR

We may fear the unknown, the unfamiliar, losing control, and what others may think of us. This fear can be so consuming we manage to convince ourselves that we're happy when we're not, or doing nothing whilst continually reminding ourselves of the worst possible outcome. Fear is like the deepest, smelliest, fart-bubbling bog that seeks to pull you into its depths and not let you go. Before you know what's happened, you're up to your neck in foul-smelling fear, oozing its way into every pore. Yuck, yuck and double yuck!

I'm here to throw you a life preserver, to help you break free. There are three steps you can start to implement right now to help you jump out of the bog of fear, and take that leap out of the comfort zone that you need to:

1. **Say *yes* before you get pulled into fear!** How many times have you dismissed opportunities before you've allowed yourself even a millisecond to consider the possibility? Or, maybe you find yourself endlessly reeling off those old familiar excuses you carry in your back pocket so you can avoid it all? When you start to say yes to all opportunities that come your way, no matter how big or small, you'll find you'll be more inclined to step out of the old comfort zone when you need to. After all, you have brought this opportunity into your life, whether you realise it or not. And, you are never given more by life than you can handle (even if you sometimes wonder). Have some faith in yourself and go for it! You may just surprise yourself.

2. **Tell fear that you want to see other people.** When you are presented with an opportunity to do something different from the norm, your fear response may be so strong that you end up running away. Or maybe you simply avoid all situations that have the potential to be unknown and/or scary (that would be literally all of them then...). Perhaps you numb and distract yourself with mindless TV watching, Internet surfing and food. Regardless of the response, it's clear that fear is most definitely trying to run the show, and you are missing out on the chance of something that could be beyond exciting and wonderful. So, here's a thought:

rather than trying to resist the fear you feel at breaking out of your comfort zone, sit with it. What you resist only persists, so try to actually face it head on. Let the fear come, and see what happens if you don't ignore it or run away from it. The more you see that fear is a by-product of your thoughts, and things are very rarely as bad as your mind can conjure up, the more fear will lessen its grip on you. Tell fear this relationship really isn't working for you; maybe suggest it goes on Tinder to find someone new?

3. **Change your story.** Maybe you've tried stepping out of your comfort zone in the past, and it was a total unmitigated disaster. Like, Hollywood disaster film carnage. It's hardly going to motivate you to want to try again. Every time someone even mentions the idea in passing you're left with nothing but feelings of dread, embarrassment, and most of all – FEAR! Maybe it's time for another story; a better one. Talk to people who have stepped away from the norm and routine who made a success of it. Read stories of people who made breaking from their comfort zone look like the most appealing and exciting thing ever. Take some time to think about all the opportunities that are out there just waiting for you to go and grab them, and allow the butterflies of excitement to flutter happily in your tummy. Don't forget to visualise yourself succeeding with the biggest grin plastered all over your beautiful face! You've got to step forward now with real belief in yourself. Be your own cheerleader, and wave your sparkle pompoms in the air like you just don't care!

There is a way to help this move out of your comfort zone go easier for you. See, our dreams are really good at staying within the confines of our mind... if we let them. You know the ones I mean – they say they'll make their dreams happen when their babies become toddlers... when their toddlers start school... when their kids leave home… when they retire… On and on with the endless excuses, and all the time their dreams are staying firmly inside their own heads whilst their life is passing them by. The way to get out of this trap, and to move your dreams into reality, is to turn your dream into a plan. You do that by making SMART goals:

S – Specific
M – Measurable
A – Attainable
R – Realistic
T – Timed

Choose a specific goal for you to focus upon. It doesn't have to be the entire dream, as this can feel too overwhelming or general for you to really focus upon. To set a specific goal, you can then look at the five 'W' factors:

- Who is involved?
- What do I want to accomplish?
- Where will it be happening?
- When will it be happening?
- Which requirements and constraints do I need to take into consideration?

You should then establish concrete criteria so that you can measure your progress towards your goal. Seeing how far you've come helps you to stay on track, as well as spurring you on to the next step of the journey. Make sure that you choose goals that you can actually reach. It's no good focusing on something that you realistically know is never going to happen; like me saying I'm going to climb Mount Everest, for example! For some people that is a goal that they can work towards and achieve, but a tortoise has more chance of getting the new 100m sprint record than I do of climbing that mountain. Setting goals that you secretly know you'll never achieve is definitely not going to make you feel happier. How can it when you'll feel like a complete failure? Ensure your goals are actually achievable for you to reach. Your goals should push you, and make effective use of the skills, abilities, financial capacity and attitudes you hold. You want to be stretched, but not so far that you snap like a tired elastic band.

The other key element is that you set yourself a time limit and stick to it. If you do all of the above but don't give yourself a set time to achieve them in, then you are making that journey so much harder for yourself. Procrastination can really play havoc with your schedule if you're not careful, and having dreams and goals without a time frame means you're more likely to drift off to something else and never make them happen. By that same token, tell people about your dreams and goals. You don't have to take an advert in the local paper or anything, but it's helpful to tell a few trusted friends or family members. They will hold you accountable for your progress, even if it's just to ask you how things are going every time they see you. Keeping it to yourself again means you can drift off, because no one will know but you!

Using SMART goals like this really puts you in a sense of control, and that in itself is a great tool for moving you out of the comfort zone. Fears can stem from the unknown, but using this method will help you to feel as though you've got more variables covered, and can thus move forward with more confidence. Coming out of your comfort zone is really a matter of you feeling secure enough to take a chance on yourself.

You've totally got this, I know you have! You can step out of the routine, the monotony and the drudge. You can break free to do something different. Grab that opportunity and know that you can be a success. I believe in you; now it's time to believe in yourself too.

Got that sunshine in my pocket

NO is a Full Sentence!

Have you ever had one of those moments when you're cornered at work by a colleague you'd rather be disco dancing with a crocodile than spend an evening with? Maybe the conversation went something like this:

Colleague: Do you fancy joining me and a couple of the girls for drinks after work?
You: Erm… yeah, sure. That'd be nice…

Inside, your mind is screaming a huge fat NO, but somehow the word seems to be lodged in your throat. So, you end up spending yet another miserable night out with people you don't like too much, rather than be cuddling up with your other half and a bottle of fizz.

Why is saying 'No' so hard?

Maybe you feel a shedload of guilt for even considering it. Maybe you can say no, but feel so bad about it that you end up giving so many justifications you end up practically losing your voice. Is 'Sorry' turning into your favourite word? Many of us are not huge fans of conflict, so we feel that by agreeing to everything that's offered to us, we can easily avoid the risk of coming to verbal blows with someone. Plus, there's the added bonus of ensuring we don't upset anyone – woe betide we say 'No' and end up with people thinking less of us. And yet, believe me when I say that saying 'Yes' all the time isn't the answer to an easy life. When you agree to everything that comes your way, all that happens is that you end up with a jam-packed schedule that makes your head spin. You'll end up feeling resentful, overtired, and hating on yourself big time.

(There's also the outcome that many don't realise – when you agree to everything, those doing the asking start to think less of you. They see you as weak and a bit of a doormat. Weird, I know, especially as you're hoping they'll like you more. Relationships truly are our greatest learning experiences!)

It's time we realised that saying 'No' can be a good thing. It saves you so much stress in the long run, and will help you to have a healthier relationship with others; and yourself. 'No' is also a full sentence, as I will explain. The work in this section may make you feel uncomfortable, but that's okay! The fact you feel this way shows that this is an issue for you, and something you would do well to face up to. It's not going to be easy, but it's definitely going to be worth it.

Let's shuffle back to the conversation we started earlier. You know, the one with the co-worker more annoying than a Dalek with PMT? Let's say you tried hard to say 'No', and rather than simply saying that and moving on with your day, you tried the well-known route of making an excuse:

Colleague: Do you fancy joining me and a couple of the girls for drinks after work?

You: Sorry, I'd love to, it's just that my brother's girlfriend's sister's cat has got the measles, and I said I'd look after him.

When you bring out this tactic, you're actually not putting her off forever. All you are doing is saying you'd love to spend time with her, but you can't do it right now and she should ask you another time. You're simply putting off the inevitable.

So, what can be done? Let's try the conversation one more time, but this time I'll show you exactly what you **should** be answering with:

Colleague: Do you fancy joining me and a couple of the girls for drinks after work?

You: No, thank you.

80

WOW!

I know, right! No stumbling over your words trying to make up some believable excuse. No red faces of dire embarrassment. No conflict, no explaining, and no panic that she's going to ask you again when she next sees you. A simple 'No, thank you' may seem too simple for words, but it's polite and to the point. Most people will take your answer and accept it without question, leaving you free to breathe easy and carry on with your life.

Most people...?

Sadly, yes. Look, I wish I could say with complete confidence that this technique was 100% guaranteed to get you out of a stinky situation every single time you tried it. How I wish it was the rainbow-coloured magic pill to solve all your problems. But, you know what life is like. There's always an exception to every rule, and there will always be that one person who won't let it lie. The one that will try to talk you out of your no, even when you've dug your feet firmly into the ground. What do we do when this skin-crawling horrible situation rises up? Well, you could resort back to the lie and excuses, but you'll have to remember to cover your tracks for the foreseeable future. Plus, you'll have the nasty taste of deceit and guilt lingering in your mouth for days.

Keeping yourself fully aligned with your 'No, thanks' will give your pursuer no power over you; there's nothing for them to latch on to and spin to make you feel guilty. If they still won't give up the ghost, you must keep strong! The only other group of people who don't like being told 'No' when they want something is children, and in that case, you have the power of the adult *'Because I said so'* to fall back on. Doing this with kids as your last resort is okay – they have to ultimately respect your decision. But, dealing with adults can prove trickier, and you aren't necessarily coming from the same advantage point. In this case, you can try:

Colleague: Do you fancy joining me and a couple of the girls for

drinks after work?
    You: No, thank you.
    Colleague: Why not?
    You: Pardon?
    Colleague: Why not?
    You: (confused) Why not what?

This tactic shows the other person that this conversation is now finished. They will either have to start the whole conversation again, or give up. If they still persist, then simply smile and resort back to the child proofing line: *'Because I said so.'*

I realise the above dialogue may make you feel like an utter cowbag. I know you're a kind and lovely person, but having boundaries *is* part and parcel of being that person. Kindness does not only extend to others, it super important to direct some at yourself too. How in the world are you supposed to give love, care and support to others if you're not looking after your own needs first? Having any kind of self-care is not selfish, including boundaries (more on that later), for you can't get water from an empty well. Having your own personal limitations ensures you're showing the love you deserve to yourself, and love to others. Perhaps the colleague that came to you (or friend/employer/family member/client) has issues with being demanding and selfish. Perhaps you being the one to finally say 'No' to them is the loving kick up the bum they need to realise what they've been doing? I can't make any promises on that front, but stranger things have happened!

The above scenario comes from not wanting to do something and not feeling overly sorry about it. You may feel guilty or anxious about causing a fuss, but there isn't deep emotional attachment underlying the problem. But, what if you need to say 'No' to someone you really love? How can you keep your boundaries in place without offending everyone?

Let's say you and your partner have finally managed to schedule some much-needed quality time together. You've both been snowed under with life recently (work, kids, running the home, etc., etc.), that you've barely said more than two words to each other in weeks. You've felt really disconnected, so you have both made the effort to make the free time for each other, so you can reconnect and have some closeness again. Wonderful stuff! Babysitter is booked, schedules are free, and your new hot to trot outfit is hanging on the wardrobe just begging to be slipped on. You feel a flutter of butterflies in your tummy that reminds you of those first flourishes of love when you first met each other, and then the phone rings:

Mum: Hello darling. I just wondered if you could possibly run me to my Zumba class tonight? The car has had to be taken into the garage, and it would really help me out.

Normally you wouldn't think twice of helping your mum; like I said, you're a lovely person. But you know in a nanosecond that you can't cancel your date with your partner. It could be weeks before you both have another chance to have an evening like this, and what kind of message is this going to be sending out to them? The call may initially set your mind into a tailspin, considering how to juggle the two commitments so that you can keep everyone happy. But, what if the traffic is bad? What if some unforeseen problem arises whilst helping your mum, and you miss the dinner reservations with your partner? Yes, you could do both – if you want to add a ton of stress to your evening, and risk ruining what sets to be a wonderful night. Either you cause a shedload of problems for yourself (and your relationship), or you tell your mum 'No'. But how to do it without hurting her feelings?

You: I'm really sorry, Mum, but I have a date with (partner's name) this evening.

Yes, I know, I know! I previously told you not to apologise or make excuses, but needs must. You have kept your explanation brief, and you haven't let your guilt drive you into a place where you try to please everyone unsuccessfully. Again, I know it isn't easy. There'll be times when you find yourself slipping back into old habits and removing yourself from your boundaries that they appear like a dot on the horizon, but it's important to keep trying. Holding the intention of being able to set clear boundaries for yourself will ensure you prioritise the important things in life, and has the added bonus of keeping your sanity in place.

There are so many demands placed upon us these days. Sometimes it feels as though we've been employed in the circus without our knowledge and we're all spinning plates. There's enough for us to stress about, so don't let anyone place unnecessary demands upon your precious time. You don't have much to spare, and that which you do have is too valuable to throw away on things you don't want to spare a second on. Make sure you say 'Yes!' to the things that excite your soul, and a polite 'No' to those that don't.

Happiness is not out there, it lies within you

Shadows Need Love Too

What if I told you that it's okay not to be okay?

You may look at me with a confused frown and scratch your head. *'But, Katie, I thought this was a book about being happy? Why are you now talking about **not** being happy?'*

You're right – this is a book about being happy. For me, learning to be happy is why we are here. It is our purpose, our main focus, the very essence of life. Happiness cannot be undervalued nor its importance underestimated. It's the very thing we're all striving for, and the intention behind every action and word. In our modern world, we need to focus on this golden emotion more than ever, and support one another to find it in our own lives. In this way, we can begin to heal ourselves and the whole world. Yes, it's **that** important!

But… (and this is *really* important, so pay attention at the back).

What if you're going through a really tragic and awful situation in your life, and happiness seems a damn near impossibility right now? Do you:

A. Bury your emotions down so deep an archaeological team couldn't find them, and paint a smile on your face so you can just pretend to be happy?
B. Try to put your focus on happiness, but every time someone asks if you're okay the masks slips and you end up bawling and snotting all over their shoulder?
C. Accept this is how you feel right now, and that's okay?

Well, ladies and gentlemen, the answer is… C.

Sometimes we all feel emotions that may not be so rainbow coloured and covered in glitter. Sometimes we can't find our smile, no matter how hard we look for it. There are days when we all feel angry, jealous of others, or downright fed up. Hell, I know I have!

Just because I can write about how to be happy, doesn't make me immune from the more negative emotions of life. My happy force field only stretches so far before life comes and stomps all over it. Case in point? I have suffered with both depression and anxiety in the past. Yes, really.

In 2012 I gave birth to my beautiful twin babies. The birth was exceedingly difficult, especially as I'd suffered with gastroenteritis for a month beforehand, and my waters went at 30 weeks. Hardly a recipe for a magical Hollywoodesque birth scene! Thank all the stars in the sky though, for they were born with relative little issues, despite being on the small side of life (they were only 3.5 pounds when they entered this world). They were both whisked off to the Special Care Baby Unit, and I was awash with the glow of post-birth exhaustion. After 4 weeks in hospital they were both allowed to come home, and life carried on – albeit with two babies added to the mix. I was (obviously) very tired, and desperately in love with my children, but…

For the first few months I felt as though I was in a permanent dense fog. My emotions seemed to be centred on a deep sadness, anxiety of both the present and the future, and strong irritability. I found it hard to sleep at night, and damn near impossible to stay awake during the day. My appetite was either ravenous enough to eat the contents of the fridge, like some towering Scooby Doo sandwich, or missing in action. I honestly thought this was how all mums with new babies felt – after all, most mums look like sleep-deprived zombies whose hormones are running wild. Surely my behaviour was normal? But, when the weeks rolled by into months, I had to hold my hands up to the fact that something was going on. Something that made me get my butt down to the doctor's; and thank goodness I did! I was suffering from postnatal depression, and was prescribed antidepressants, which put me back on the right track in no time at all.

During those foggy months, I genuinely felt as though I'd never smile again. I'm not exaggerating for effect here; the weight of my own depression was suffocating. In that moment, if someone had told me just to get on with it and get happy, I probably would've slapped them, cried on their shoulder, or both! At that time, I was feeling both depressed and anxious, and that's okay. That was how I felt, and I dealt with it in a way that allowed me to move through it and come out the other side. I want to stress though that you don't have to be suffering with depression to not be in a happy place; it doesn't have to be such an extreme situation, but that doesn't make your situation any less important. There are days even now when I'm less than happy and find it hard to get my joyful groove on. This isn't because there's anything 'wrong' with me either – it makes me human.

Part of being a human being upon this planet is having a side to ourselves that we are less than proud of. A part of us that we are embarrassed of, that we push down, ignore and pretend doesn't exist: our shadow side. The term 'shadow' was first used by psychologist Carl G. Jung in 1912 to describe the denied or repressed aspects of the self. And this repression starts at such a young age! Many children start to hide parts of themselves when they are told (wrongly) that these parts are unacceptable:

- *'Sit quietly.'*
- *'Children are seen and not heard.'*
- *'Big boys don't cry.'*
- *'Why can't you just be good?'*
- *'Stop acting out!'*
- *'Stop making a scene!'*
- *'Why can't you be like all the other boys and girls?'*

On and on it goes, like some never-ending conveyor belt of crap, eating away at our sense of self. Anything that's deemed 'bad' becomes akin to the monster under the bed, and we hide it away in the hope that no one will ever see that the monster looks like us. Into adulthood we trot, our secret monsters dutifully following behind. We never look at them, but we sense their presence in the background of our lives, and they can really shape the person we are. At its core, our shadow self is the collective name given to aspects of selves we don't take ownership of because of fear. For, at a subconscious level, we worry if people knew the truth of all of who we are, we'd be judged, rejected or thrown out.

Have you ever had that moment where you suddenly realised that someone may inadvertently see your shadow? Maybe you were having a full-on tantrum at the photocopier for jamming for the hundredth time that day, and someone walked in on you. Or maybe, you were a sobbing, snotty mess of jealousy, bawling your eyes out in a toilet cubicle, when a kindly stranger passed you some tissue under the door. Whatever the scenario, the idea that someone may see the 'real us' should be a gateway to real connections with others, based on compassion and authenticity; and sometimes that happens. But, most of the time, this notion of being 'caught out' is enough to send you down the rabbit warren of panic, shame and fear. As though you need to only show your good side to be liked by other people! When did emotions become so categorised anyway? Who was it that decided that one emotion was bad, whilst another was good? Labelling them in this way only leads to enough guilt to sink a formidable boat that's about to crash and sink Leonardo DiCaprio and Kate Winslet! Emotions are your mind's way of reacting to a situation. They are not in themselves good or bad, but it's our interpretation of them that really messes things up.

When life shows up and decides to give us a sharp slap around the face, we feel as though we're expected to respond in a certain way: smile; think positive thoughts; kick that fear to the curb! And sometimes, that is exactly what you need to do. After all, living in a negative world indefinitely is going to do nothing but pull you down and keep you stuck. But, being afraid of our shadow can lead to a world of difficulties too. By being open to exploring this part of ourselves in healthy ways, we can actually release an enormous amount of personal and creative power. We can become all we ever wished to be!

And, if we look to deny ourselves this dive into all we are, we put ourselves and others in danger of the shadow side of our nature exploding out like some spewing volcano. Hurt people hurt people. They may lash out in the belief that doing so protects them from getting hurt, or their behaviour could be an unconscious projection of the issues they refuse to face. Regardless of the reason, this denial of self can really end up hurting a lot of people; something that has no basis in happiness whatsoever.

So, yes, this book is focused on happiness, and how you can take control of your own happiness in each and every moment. I'm a huge fan of joy and positivity, and I know they have the power to change lives. But it is vital to note that we need to be in the right head space to work on our happiness. If you're not, it may be the last thing on your radar. Or it may seem like a mere speck on the horizon. And that's okay! That is actually a very real and tangible part of most people's experiences. Like I said before, no one is happy all the time (not even little old me), and we all have times where happiness seems very far away. In that space, what do we do?

Learning how to become mindful and truly present with our feelings in any given moment allows us to delve into the world of authentic self-exploration and self-expression. Without choosing to look at ourselves for all we are, the emotions within us can run wild; causing havoc in countless unthinkable ways. But, the moment we identify them and call them out is the moment we give ourselves access to our own personal power. Jealousy, for example, can be seen as being pretty toxic, but left unchecked, it can potentially grow into something far darker where people end up getting hurt. By taking the time to call out how we're feeling, we create space to see it for what it is, and the reasons behind those feelings. We then have a stronger platform to decide whether we wish to continue with that feeling, or whether we consciously want to shift it to something more positive. The simple act of creating that space will give you the time to do that, should you wish to. Many more fearful emotions rage unchecked in the moment, without you stopping to consider whether it's a good idea. By simply taking a moment to stop, think and breathe, you may find yourself naturally moving away from such extreme reactions, to something more thoughtful and considered.

Be aware too that language has power. The words you use to describe how you're feeling will give you greater power to ascertain why you feel that way; the root cause of it all. So, if you're feeling in a positive place, try to avoid use of the blanket term of 'good'. Are you content, loved, joyful, appreciated, or satisfied, for example? In that same vein, when you're not in a good place, try to find a more descriptive word than just 'bad'. Consider whether you are confused, lost, afraid, or inadequate, for example. Words matter. Words have incredible power. By being specific, you will be able to help yourself in the act of real self-exploration.

You have to understand that it's not just the seemingly negative thoughts and feelings that hide in your shadows that have an effect on you; if only it were that simple! So many of us are raised to be the happy child (don't make a fuss/stop crying/don't make a scene/be good) that we see anything less than that as something to be deeply ashamed of. We place such high expectations on ourselves of how we're supposed to feel, it's insane. Guilt and shame are literal weights on our shoulders that push us down and keep us from reaching for the happiness that's rightly ours. Indeed, the feelings about our feelings can make us feel worse than the original negativity; talk about piling rubbish on rubbish! Making the loving and non-judgemental space to acknowledge the feelings that are currently circulating around your mind without feeling bad shame about them is a good start to finding peace within and without.

Of course, it doesn't help that your loved ones have such a strong reaction to anything less than you being happy. Their worry and fear about you can also cause you a shedload of guilt that you're responsible for them feeling bad. But it can be really hard for them to see you feeling bad, because they care so much about you. That and the fact that they are deeply uncomfortable with anything that's seen as painful and challenging. The human response is to kick into 'fix a feeling' mode, and they'll do all they can to try and help make things better for you. Sometimes this is okay – you're ready to move on to a more positive mindset, and you appreciate their help in making this happen. But, sometimes you're not ready for a different feeling, even if it is a better or more helpful one than the emotions that are currently taking up residency in your head. You are not here to manage how other people feel. There's enough responsibility looking after your own mental and emotional health without spending all your time trying to make everyone else happy too. Your work is to be honest with yourself, and to become comfortable in your own skin. Let your loved ones focus on their shadow side, even if they do come to you with love and concern. They can't fix you; that's your job.

If it all becomes too much, you can always use the phrase: *'I'm processing right now, thank you for asking.'* That tells your loved one that you're still working through your feelings, but it doesn't automatically dismiss their concerns either. Right now, you're are sitting with certain emotions, but that's okay, for nothing lasts forever. When the processing is done, you may be ready to move on to something better.

In that same vein, be aware of how you talk to yourself too. Getting guilt from others is one thing, but it doesn't begin to compare with the things you say to yourself. It's all too easy to heal on a shallow level, and pretend to ourselves that we're okay now. After all, the initial pains have been fixed now, and that's enough, right? We don't need to worry about the causes of that pain, so long as we're alright in the short term and aren't making ourselves feel awful for not being okay. But there's nothing wrong with not being okay; it doesn't make you a bad person. You don't genuinely believe that every other person is happy all the time, do you? That everyone else knows what they're doing all the time? You don't feel super shiny smiley right now, and that's not something to mentally beat yourself up over. Bring yourself back to what's going on inside, and tell yourself, *'I'm feeling _____ right now, and that's okay.'* Tell yourself that you're not doing anything wrong, and your mind will start to accept it so you can start to work through it.

Don't be afraid of getting super honest with the darkness though. If you have a relationship in your life that you know can sustain an honest conversation without them falling into the 'fix a feeling' mode, then opening up could be the best thing you could ever do. To have someone that just listens and holds the space for your honesty – all the rawness and reality of that – can really help you to make sense of what's happening within you. Don't hold them accountable for making it better for you; by giving you the safe space to talk, they're allowing you to explore and find your own healing. These people are rare, and if you have one in your life you should cherish them; they're a real gift in delving into the shadow side of your own nature.

Another way to shed some light on your shadows is through a Murk, Muck and Me Ritual. What the hell is a Murk, Muck and Me Ritual, I hear you cry? Well, I'll tell you!

Murk, Muck and Me Ritual

Find a quiet space where you won't be disturbed for a while. This means no TV, no kids, no phones… nothing. Just you and the peace and quiet.

Light a candle and take several deep breaths all the way down into your belly.

Stare into the flame of the lighted candle and mentally ask yourself – *'How am I feeling right now?'*

Pay attention to any thoughts, feelings or physical symptoms that arise (tight shoulders or a rumbly tummy, for example). Don't automatically dismiss anything out of hand, even if it makes no sense right now.

Write down everything that showed up as an answer to your question – ALL OF IT.

Turn your findings into something creative. This could be a piece of writing in the form of a letter to the feelings or a poem; a painting; drawing; or a collage. Tap into your creativity and express your feelings.

The idea behind this is that you are honouring these feelings rather than burying them again. By doing this, you are more likely to accept the shadow side of yourself and be able to sit with it, rather than automatically running in the opposite direction. You are made up of so many glorious and complex things, and not all of them are shiny and smiley. Getting familiar with the darkness will help you to do something you may have always strived for, but never quite achieved it in the past: accept all of who you are.

The other thing to bear in mind about your shadow is that every aspect of your life is there to teach you something, and this is no exception. Your supposed 'negative' emotions can tell you an awful lot about yourself and what's going on with you. For example:

- Bitterness shows you where you need to focus your healing, and where you're still holding judgements towards yourself and others.
- Resentment signifies that you are living in the past rather than accepting the past to be what it is.
- Discomfort is a huge message for you to pay attention to what is happening right now, as you're being given the chance to change how you approach things, and do things differently to how you normally would.
- Anger points to the things that you're really passionate about, where your boundaries are, and what you feel needs to change in the world.
- Disappointment shows that you reached for something. You

tried rather than simply giving in to apathetic tendencies, and you still care deeply.

- Guilt points to the fact that you're living in the shadow of others' expectations of your life.
- Shame signifies that you've internalised how other people believe how you should live or who you should be, rather than connecting to your own inner guidance.
- Anxiety points to the fact that you're either stuck in the past, or in deep fear of the future. It's an internal sign for you to wake up and be present; like an inner kick up the bum.
- Sadness shows just how much you care, about others and the world. It signifies the size of your beautiful heart.

When doing shadow work to explore this side of yourself so that you may gain greater self-awareness and acceptance of all that you are, know that it's going to kick up stuff that may make you feel super uncomfortable. It's called your shadow for a reason, and you're not going to find magical unicorns and fluffy kittens hiding in there! Create a safe space for yourself to do this work, if you feel drawn to it. You're heading off on an exploration that most people are too scared to go on, and it's not going to be the easiest of adventures. You don't need the added worry of what others may think of you on top of all that. So find a space where you can have the time and room to do what you need to without any pressure or anxiety from external sources. Go gently with yourself, one baby step at a time. Bring in an essence of playful curiosity, and try not to let fear run the show. You're already stepping into the darkness of who you are and you don't want to head off into that place without your light of love leading the way. If all gets too much, step back. Take a break from the work and reconnect with the more positive aspects of yourself. There's no time limit on this, and it doesn't have to be done in one go. Indeed, like all aspects of looking at and knowing yourself, it's a lifelong journey that's full of surprises, revelations and epiphanies. Don't think you're going to have it all done in time for your favourite television show!

A trusted confidante or therapist can really help you if you find it difficult at any point to do this on your own. Journaling has always been a huge part of my shadow work, and my journal is akin to a private diary for me. It's not for others to gawp at and find my secrets, but it's for me to really get to grips with all aspects of who I am in a free and unedited flow. Within its pages I have free written about the things that really niggle at me; investigated recurring aspects of my shadow; defining memories; explored dreams; deconstructed blockages; and looked at what's triggering me. I've even dialogued with my shadow directly, asking her how I can accept her and bring her more fully into my life. Each time I turn to my journal I learn more about myself. I accept myself. I love myself. It's like a journey back to myself; to make myself whole.

Another practice that has really worked for me is meditation. Meditating can seem really daunting to those who haven't done it before, but you don't have to be a Buddhist monk chanting 'Ohm' on a mountaintop to get it right! At its core, meditation is making space to be with yourself, without distraction. The breath is the key, and by drawing your full attention to this, you'll be able to create the room to become truly mindful and present. You can never stop your chattering monkey mind, but it doesn't mean you have to give your full attention to every thought that rolls in. In a meditative state, you'll quickly realise that you are not your thoughts, but the spaces in between them; for your thoughts come of their own accord. For shadow work, you will see that your shadow self will naturally begin to surface over a period of time. You then will have the safe space in order to both acknowledge and accept what comes up. Though again, if it becomes too overwhelming, you always have the power to stop. You are always in control of delving into your shadow, and can move back whenever you choose. Don't let the fear of all the potential bad things that could happen from doing this work (which are so unlikely, you've got more chance of winning the Lottery) stop you from doing what could be the most rewarding thing you ever do.

Also pay attention to someone who really triggers you and gets under your skin. We all have them, no matter how much you try to see the good in everyone around you. But, here's the thing (and I'm sorry, but you're not going to like this), they are a reflection of you. The characteristics that a person holds that are winding you up so much might actually be a mirror to something within your own shadow that you haven't addressed yet. By drawing your attention to them and getting so worked up about it, it's actually a sign from yourself to step back and see what's happening within. What you see without is all a reflection of within.

Shadow work is immensely powerful stuff. You are consciously tapping into sides of yourself that have been repressed; maybe for years. By shining your light on them, you have the potential to unleash a real dynamic force from within, which in turn can bring lasting changes in both your consciousness and your life. Shadow work is transformational, and you will never be able to go back to the person you were before you started looking at yourself for all that you are. Get real and face each emotion as it arises in each moment. The stronger and more repressed the emotion, the more it can surface for you in really intense and uncomfortable ways until you hold it up fully to the light and give it the same love and respect that you do for all the other more 'positive' emotions within you. Think of yourself as a beautiful onion, carefully peeling back the layers to reveal the true heart within. Don't rip the outer layers off with force and pain; they all make you who you are, and are all equally important.

Don't expect it to be an overnight job either. Shadow work takes time, because the stuff you're uncovering has practically been engraved on your brain. But know that whatever has been constructed within can also be deconstructed, should you make the time and effort to do so. We all have a shadow; it's nothing to be ashamed of. You can't run away from it either; for wherever you go, you will always find yourself. But the shadow does contain positive qualities too. For example, let's say you uncover that at times you can come across as being too uncaring and quite cold. Initially, this may make you feel deeply ashamed, and even disgusted with yourself; but it's not all bad. You are actually not serving yourself when you're not being clear about your boundaries, and identifying this part of your shadow helps you to see that you need to learn to honour your own needs and know when to say no. Through looking at your shadow, it can actually help you live a happier and more positive life!

Ultimately, if you feel that you're simply pretending to have positive emotions, thoughts and feelings on a regular basis, this can actually block your growth and evolution. Suppressing any more negative emotion, whether that be anger, fear or jealousy, only feeds the shadow and leaves you with more work to do! Remember to stick two fingers up to labelling any emotion as being 'good' or 'bad'; for it's only your own interpretation that defines them as such.

It's time to be real, authentic and true to who we are. It's time to love ourselves, no matter how we might be feeling. Send love to every single part of you – the light and the dark. Know that you deserve to be loved, and you deserve to be happy. And that means accepting and loving all that you are.

Come home to yourself.

Happiness is always knocking at your door, you just have to let it in

Once Upon a Time

Once upon a time there was a young girl who lived what looked like a charmed life. She had a family that loved her, and friends who she shared her secrets and her giggles with. She was bright enough to attend an all-girls grammar school in her hometown, and had a wide variety of interests outside of the classroom. The young girl should've been happier than a sand boy at the beach. She should have had the confidence and belief to chase her dreams and live life to the fullest. After all, everyone told her how clever and pretty she was. Surely the path ahead should've been paved with rainbows, unicorns and fairies.

But the young girl had a problem... she didn't believe she could. In her eyes she wasn't clever enough, amazing enough, or unique enough to go after what she really wanted. She told herself she would fail if she tried, so what was the point? The story she told herself was that people wouldn't really like her unless she did everything in her power to be the nicest, funniest girl she could possibly be; as well as doing whatever it was that they wanted to do. And so it went that the girl ended up doing a qualification that she didn't really want to do, because she didn't believe she could be successful at what she actually loved. The young girl also found herself in doomed relationship after doomed relationship, each with a man more unsuitable than the last. She was bullied at school, no matter how much she tried to fit in and be like the popular crowd she so desperately wanted to belong to. The girl could never really understand why her life wasn't the magical adventure that she'd been told it would be. She couldn't for the life of her understand what she was doing wrong. It all seemed so desperately unfair...

Hands up if you figured out that I'm the sad heroine of the tale? Yes, I'm sad to say that young girl was me. I was the one who should've been able to have the best of what life had to offer; at least that's what I'd always been told. And yet, somehow, it didn't work out that way, but it took me another 15 years or so to figure out why! See, many believe themselves to be some kind of prisoner of their own mind. A slave to their thoughts. But nothing could be further from the truth. Your mind only believes what you tell it over and over again. If you focus on anything for any period of time, your mind will accept that as being your reality; regardless of whether it's true or not. The stories you then tell yourself have a direct impact on your life.

Let me give you an example. Let's say a young man shows real talent at football. His family and his school encourage him in this talent every step of the way, and push him to go for extra training and competitions. As he sees his skills develop, and the accolades come in, his confidence and self-esteem skyrocket, which in turn motivate him to keep pushing forward with his dream. He believes he is good at football right down into his core, and doesn't see any reason why his dream of becoming a professional footballer wouldn't happen. And, sure enough, he ends up getting signed with a football club. He has the skill and support, but it's his own story that he can do this that helps him be where he wants to be. For without that positive story, all the skill in the world wouldn't help him get there. He would stop himself before he gave himself even half a chance.

Let's say that your life isn't what you'd like it to be. Maybe you have dreams in the back of your mind, but you stop yourself from making them a reality because you don't believe in yourself enough to go for it. What can you do to flip this around, and start to actually live your life to the fullest? Well, the first step to changing any limited belief is to identify it. For nothing is going to really shift unless you call it out for what it is. And yes, it's going to make you feel super uncomfortable – but that's a good thing! Feeling that way shows you that you're doing something that you know isn't that great for you. You don't need to get all judgemental on yourself as you identify it, by the by. There's no point in taunting yourself for telling a story based off low self-esteem; hardly likely to turn things around for you! All that's going to do is add more negativity to your story and put you even further back from where you want to be! Identify it, yes, but don't hate yourself for it.

Once you've identified the story you're telling yourself on loop, the next step is to change it to something more positive. Like I said, your mind only believes what you tell it to be true, so if your story is holding you back you **always** have the power to change it. The difference between you wanting to be a successful entrepreneur, famous actor, published writer (or whatever your dream is) and the people who are actually doing it is the story. And it's time to counter the conveyer belt of crap that is like a ticker tape to your daily life.

Examples? Let me show you:

FROM
'Everything I've done so far has failed.'
TO
'Things haven't worked out so far because I was focusing on the wrong things, but now I know what's right for me.'

FROM
'Every relationship I've been in has been a disaster. I swear I only attract people that treat me badly.'
TO
'I deserve love, and to be relationships based on understanding, trust and compassion. I welcome this into my life with an open heart.'

FROM
'I'm so bad with my finances! I never have enough money, and I'm always broke.'
TO
'I take responsibility for my finances. I make sound financial

decisions, and I am able to budget within my means.'

Get the idea? You change the words you tell yourself, the focus and the energy behind your story. It all becomes more rooted in positivity, which in turn will help you to create a happy life. But, we need to go a step further, because the story isn't always enough. The words need to be anchored to something tangible so that your mind is more likely to accept what you're telling it. It takes 90 days to form new pathways in the brain – new beliefs and realities. 90 days of consistent reaffirming and storytelling, but if you root it in something real, this process can be both quicker and easier. How do you do this? Visualisation.

Let's take the footballer again. Let's say that he was practising his skills every day and dreaming of being a professional, but he still had doubts that it would actually happen. He tries to change his story to feature on positive belief, but his mind fights against the new reality. So he adds in that little bit extra – he starts to visualise himself scoring the winning goal at Wembley in front of thousands of cheering fans. Every single time he repeats his positive story, he visualises this scene inside his mind. He imagines how that moment will feel: the excitement, the adrenalin, the suspense. And the more he does this, the more his mind accepts his story as true – he is a professional footballer! Now, it's simply a matter of time before the opportunity goes from visualisation to real life experience!

Now of course, it's worth pointing out that the magic of manifesting isn't necessarily instantaneous. It's not a case of creating a new story, doing the visualisations, and then suddenly you have the dream in a blink of an eye. It could happen that way, but it might not. And if the magic doesn't zoom in like some sparkly thunderbolt, that doesn't mean that it won't come in at all. This process does require patience, as well as a huge heap of faith that you deserve to have your dreams come true, and they will. But what this work does do is that it opens you up to opportunities that you may have completely passed by before; either because you were too submerged in your own negativity, or because you didn't feel worthy of them. Now you'll find that you have the courage and drive to actually grab them with both hands, and when you do so you'll find that they could just be that magical moment that makes your dreams come true. So please don't be angry with yourself or the Universe that what you're affirming isn't happening fast enough for you, or the changes don't come all in one go. Taking small steps in the direction of your dreams every single day will put you where you want to be, if you're consistent. Don't beat yourself up if you find yourself falling back into the old habits of negative storytelling; you're human, it happens. Just take a deep breath, dust yourself off, and bring yourself back to your positive story.

Just one more little note about making a new story for yourself – be careful of saying you're just as good as anyone else. See, the ego can't help but want to come in and mess things up for you, if you give it room to do so. It'll latch on to that 'anyone else' part of the message faster than customers grabbing a free sample of chocolate at the supermarket. The minute you bring in any kind of comparison to anyone else, even if it's done indirectly, you'll start to see yourself as not being as good as them. Rather than heading down this path to unhappiness, switch it to 'I'm good/great/ amazing at…' The only competition you need to have in your life is the person looking back at you in the mirror!

If you're going to indulge in an inner fantasy world of dreams and wishes (as we all do), then why wouldn't you choose a positive one for yourself? Consider this: do your stories help move you forward? If not, it's time to consider leaving them behind and move on to something more uplifting and useful. After all, this is your life, and you deserve to make it the best possible one you can, for you! It's time to get happy!

No one is in charge of your happiness except you

Stop Being a Drama Llama

Let me ask you a question:
Are you a drama llama?

What do I mean by that? Well, do you create issues and tensions in every area of your life, and secretly thrill in it? Do you wade in to your friends' problems, even when they have nothing to do with you? Do you find yourself bored by life, and are constantly searching for drama to make it more exciting?

Then, I'm sorry to break it to you, but you may be addicted to drama. You may, in fact, be a drama llama.

In essence, we all have that side to us. Who doesn't thrill in the latest celebrity gossip over who's fallen out with who? Who secretly love it when your friend fills you on all their latest shenanigans? Listening to other people's issues and dramas can be really entertaining at times, no matter how guilty we may feel for revelling in the drama. But, actually, drama serves little purpose. All it really does is create stress and tension; neither of which are particularly healthy for you. And, when you're a drama llama, you're deliberately choosing to expose yourself to these feelings every single day. You can see how it can start to have a real negative impact on your overall sense of well-being!

It's worth noting that I'm not immune from this either. For years, I religiously bought celebrity gossip magazines every week. I couldn't get enough of the scandals and the high drama. But, after around three years or so, it hit me like a steam train: I don't actually know these people, neither do I know if what's being printed is actually true! The media is great at printing stories that are based on the merest hint of evidence, or even fabricated altogether. Besides, after reading them, I could feel myself sinking lower into a pool of negativity. These magazines were hardly the stuff of inspiration and empowerment; they were actually making me feel really rubbish about myself. So, I vowed there and then not to buy them ever again; not to conspire in the whirlwind of drama. That was in 2011, and the positive effect has been huge. Don't get me wrong, I'm not suddenly immune from showing an interest in the goings-on of celebrities if I hear it, but I don't consciously gorge myself on it like I used to. I made the choice to step back from my own obsession with drama, and you can too.

It's time to get honest with yourself, from a place of love and non-judgement. After all, there's no point in doing this if you're only going to start critically finger-pointing at yourself; that's only going to be bringing more drama to the table! If we really want to make the changes in our lives, we need be self-reflective, but to keep showing ourselves love throughout.

So… do you have high levels of drama in multiple areas of your life? Is the relationship with your partner more on and off than a traffic light? Do you find yourself continually in trouble at work, and don't stop moaning about your boss? Do you have consistent arguments with your friends? If these questions are making you squirm in embarrassment, let me ask you another question: are you creating all of this? See, we don't tend to do things unless there's something in it for us. So, what's the pay-off from all this drama for you? Maybe you feel stuck in a rut in your life, and you're looking to create some excitement. Perhaps you feel neglected and left out of things, and so you inadvertently seek attention from others. Even if it's negative attention, it's got to be better than no attention, right? Or, maybe you grew up in a household where drama was the norm for you, and so you only feel truly comfortable if you're surrounded by it. If you see yourself in these, then it's time to consider alternative solutions. For example, if you are looking to get attention from others, can you do it a way that's more positive and direct rather than being passively aggressive? If you're bored and fed up with your life, what adventures can you create to move you forward? By identifying the reasons behind your drama llama behaviour, you can then take back control of your life and see how you can make positive changes.

We get back what we put out into the world. Your intention really is your calling card, so we draw to us the things we find ourselves continually focusing on. If your inner world is one of drama, stress and negativity, you can hardly be surprised if you attract people who come with the same energy! You are way more powerful than you give yourself credit for, and the changes you seek in life all start within you. So, look to change your perspective. Focus your mind on what you are grateful for, and find happiness in the little things in life. When you consciously look for things to be happy about, you'll start to find more and more and your mind will shift to a more positive outlook. Lots of the drama in our lives actually takes place within our own minds, after all. Rarely is it about what's actually going on around you, but more about your own perspective towards the situation. Let me give you an example:

Let's say you're at work. The woman who sits opposite you is going through a really hard time at home, but is doing her best to keep her private life private; or so she thinks. Rather than being open with others, her behaviour has spiralled down with stress to become short-tempered and highly strung. She shouts at the slightest thing, and seems to have no patience with anyone. You don't know what's happening at home, and you take her behaviour really personally. Rather than seeking to reach out to her with compassion and understanding, you create a whirlwind of negativity inside your own mind –

'What a cow! How dare she speak to me like that! Who does she think she is anyway?'

You then retaliate to the belief that her behaviour is aimed at you, even though it's not, and you start to fire back your own torpedoes of vileness, and missiles of hate. Although your co-worker's initial crappy behaviour wasn't about you, it certainly is now! She hits back at you, and before you know where you are, battle lines have been drawn and there's a full-scale conflict taking place. And, all because you created a drama llama story inside your own mind rather than lovingly asking her if she was okay.

Sound familiar?

You have power over this situation, and it's this: just be. Consider whether it may be a good idea to try speaking less, and actually listening more. After all, we have two ears and only one mouth (way too many people seem to have that concept mixed up in their own heads too; at least by how much they seem to like the sound of their own voice anyway). When someone starts to wave their own drama llama flag, try not to react to it. Observe them, and consider why they may be behaving in this way. Oh, and please resist the urge to jump into a pity party with someone. Drama flipping loves company, and the drama llama will inadvertently do their best to get someone else to join them in their drama waving. Surely if there's someone who agrees with them, then that justifies the drama, right? Wrong! Step back and let said individual get on with it – this isn't your party, and you don't need to bring balloons.

On that note, be slow to label anything as being a 'drama'. Labels stick harder than dried egg on a plate, and sometimes what we're labelling is just someone who needs our love and attention. Remember when I said negative attention can be seen as being better than no attention at all? Maybe the drama llama in your life doesn't want a full-scale fight; maybe they just need a hug and a friendly ear. Just a thought. Situations themselves aren't 'bad' or 'good' – it's our own interpretation of them that makes them that way. Just focus on being there for someone with love and compassion. Let the drama go.

If there is someone in your life who is consistently immersed in drama no matter how much love and support you give them, it may be time to reconsider the relationship. It's hard, but these kinds of unhealthy connections will only leave you feeling stressed and unhappy. Take an inventory of which people leave you feeling miserable after they've left your company. Consider whether you'd be better off removing these people from your life. If you can't, then look to minimise the time you do have to be with them. If you have to keep a drama llama in your life, then start to look for triggers that send them spiralling down the drama path, and look to steer the conversation away to something more positive when you notice them. It may be tough, especially at first, but you'll be doing both of you the biggest favour you can think of in the long run.

Also look to be straight with people. The breeding ground of drama is gossip, and a lot of that comes from misunderstandings or overreactions. Start to say exactly what you mean with people, and let them know they can be honest with you. If you're someone who has trouble with being assertive, this may be hard at first. But, I promise you, the first time you have to do it will be the hardest. The more you do it, the easier it becomes. And, rather a short space of discomfort than a huge shedload of drama that could well up. When done with love, honesty really is the best policy.

Finally, when drama does come into your life (which it will; life is full of it), see what you can learn from the situation. Accept it, learn from it, and then get on with your life. Don't give more attention than absolutely necessary to these situations, and know they can always help us to move forward. After all, life will always involve mini fires that we feel desperate to put out. But, if we can learn not to fan them, they may actually be able to light our way.

Don't put the keys to your happiness is someone else's pocket

Let it All Go

Do you carry a wardrobe upon your back? Not literally of course, but a sense that you're carrying around a huge weight of stuff that you really ought to put down?

Guilt
Shame
Unforgiveness
Hurt
Anger
Jealousy
Unworthiness
Resentment
Fear

All of these have one thing in common: they're all really bad for us. They stop us moving forwards with our lives; stop us doing what we really want to do; and stop us being happy. And yet, we carry them around with us like some old, tattered comfort blanket. And, why? Because we believe they're part of our story. We feel justified in carrying them with us because we have done for so long. If we did let them go, what then? Let me tell you, by letting all this crap go you can make room in your life for the good stuff, and I'm going to tell you how.

First off, let's start by examining each of the issues in turn which we may be carrying around with us, and why they are bad for us:

1. Trying to control everything
The only thing you are truly in control of is yourself; your own reactions and attitudes. You can't control what someone else may do, say or feel. Yes, you can make it easier for that person to be happy, to love, and to be kind, but you can't force them to!

112

Sometimes you really do just have to let life happen the way it's supposed to. Stressing about the way you want things to go isn't helping anyone, and certainly not you. Trying to relax and letting things flow can actually provide surprising results that you would have never even dreamed of. Control yourself yes, but try to let go of the need to control everything else.

2. Being a people pleaser

I was a chronic people pleaser for years! Like, YEARS! My self-esteem was so low that I genuinely thought it was important to put others' needs before my own, or else they wouldn't like me. Yes, I'm aware of how crazy that sounds. And yet, I'm not the only one to engage in people-pleasing activity; far from it. But, let me ask you this: why are other people more important than you? When did your needs become so unimportant? When you're a people pleaser, you take a giant step back from yourself and what makes you happy. You're so focused on making the other person smile, you lose sight of whether what you're doing is actually what *you want*. Because, ultimately, this is your life, and it's up to you to make it the best life you can for you. By letting go of the obsessive need to people please you start to focus more on your own needs and happiness, which in turn will help put you where you want to be.

3. Sense of entitlement

I hate to burst your bubble, but no one is going to knock on your front door and hand you all your dreams on a plate. Neither do you necessarily deserve the breaks more than the next person. We are all deserving of love, happiness and abundance – but it's up to us to go out into the world and make it happen. If you become the backseat passenger of your own life, how on earth do you hope to be in control of your own destiny? By that same token, when crappy things happen to you (which they will; life can be like that), you may find yourself asking, *'Why me?'* But, why **not** you?

Everyone has gets their share of joy and sorrow weaved through their life, and you aren't above this. You do deserve happiness, but you're not immune from life and *all* it offers. Besides, sometimes our challenges can be our biggest lessons.

4. Resentment

When you carry the flame of anger and resentment within you, it does nothing but eat you up from the inside out. If someone has wronged you in some way, you need to find a way to make peace with that. I'm not saying that what they did to you was okay; it wasn't. We're not condoning bad behaviour here; it's about swapping pain for our own sense of peace. When you carry around resentment, you are allowing the person who hurt you to still have power over your life, and I know you don't want that to happen. Sometimes the best thing we can do for our own souls is to accept an apology we never actually received.

5. Guilt

I have this thing as a parent: I'm guilty all the time. No matter what I do, or don't do, I carry around a huge knot of guilt in my stomach that it's not enough; there's always more that I could be doing. I'm basically damned if I do and I'm damned if I don't. And yet, we are all just trying our best. Mentally beating yourself up about that isn't going to change anything. What is better for you is to be proactive if you feel there's a call for you to do so. If you're being lazy and procrastinating, maybe there is more that you can do. In that case, let go of the guilt and get your bum off the sofa! If you've made mistakes along the way, take responsibility for them. Apologise where necessary, and see what you can do to make things better. Let go of guilt, and take control.

6. Pride

Yes, be proud of all that you are – your achievements, your triumphs, your bravery. But don't let pride cloud your vision so much that it stops you leading a full and happy life. When pride rules the roost, you can't apologise or forgive with any sense of sincerity. When pride is in charge, close relationships will suffer, because there's a brick wall in the way of your bond. The old saying of 'pride comes before a fall' is not some old wives' tale; it has its roots in truth. Don't let your own pride trip you up.

7. Perfectionism

If you strive for perfection, you'll end up feeling disappointed, judgemental and hopeless. Human beings weren't born to be perfect. We make mistakes, we have flaws. To pretend otherwise is putting yourself on the road to misery. Perfection rises up from a place of control and low self-esteem, and we've seen how both of these things won't bring you happiness. The perfect partner/friend/co-worker/family member doesn't exist. No matter what their role in your life, we have to do our best to accept people for who they are, and love them as such. Coming to any relationship with a checklist and an improvement plan will only make the other person feel as though they're not good enough, and will spoil the chance of a strong and loving connection. And, just as there's no such thing as a perfect person, neither is there the reality of a perfect life. Your life is a result of the things that you put into it and the choices you make on every step of that journey. No matter what life brings, it's up to you to make it the best version of life that makes *you* happy.

8. Negativity

When we sit, and focus our thoughts and words on complaining and what's wrong with our lives, we are literally putting out a call to the Universe to ask for more of the same. Yes, I know that sounds bonkers, but the Law of Attraction is a powerful thing. You can inadvertently create more reasons to complain, even though that's the last thing you want! Compared to millions of others across the world, you have so many reasons to be grateful and happy; but it's up to you to see this. Doing what you can to move your mind to a more positive outlook can actually create more reasons to be happy. Anything is possible if you want it bad enough.

9. Unhealthy relationships

You are the culmination of the main 5 people in your life. So, if you surround yourself with toxic, draining and negative people, you can hardly expect to have an abundance of happiness for yourself. Letting go of people is probably the hardest thing to do on this list, and yet it can prove to be the most liberating act you can ever do. By that same token, try not to dwell too much on your past relationships. You broke up with this person for a reason, and focusing your thoughts on what might have been can stop you having the fulfilling and happy relationship you deserve with someone else. If your thoughts do drift to them, try to focus on the lessons that relationship gave you, and wish them well. Allow both of you to move on with your lives; for we all deserve to be happy.

10. Being busy all the time

We live in a society that seems to equate being busy with achievement, which in turn leads to happiness. So, we find ourselves pushed to fill up every waking hour, to be on the go 24/7, and to multitask ourselves into a stress. But, this path will ultimately lead to nothing but feeling strung out, overworked, miserable and exhausted. Hardly a recipe for being happy! Yes, our lives require us to meet obligations, but it's also important to have quiet times where we unplug and relax. Balance is key.

11. An attachment to money

We all have basic needs, and these deserve to be met. But, once you have reached this point, it's important to consider whether the trade-off for earning more and more is really worth it. See, most of us have the dream of being millionaires, but unless you win the lottery, it requires hard work, long hours, and total dedication to the pursuit of that goal. For some, it may be worth it, but many will feel the pressure to not be worth the effort and the negative impact it'll have on their life. What's more important is to find work that makes your heart sing with joy; your passion and your happiness. When you allow this to be your focus, the money will be the cherry on the cake, without dominating your life.

12. Fear of failure

No one is immune from failure, and if you've ever put yourself out there, chances are it hasn't worked out for you at some point. Did you keel over from the situation? No, you didn't, and yet many are so terrified that they might fail that it stops them doing anything at all. The risk of failure will never go away, but it's really important to feel the fear and do it anyway! When we're brave enough to try, we could actually create something truly magical for ourselves. If failure is a possibility, so is success; but you won't know until you try. The fear of failure can show itself in many ways too. Excuses is a key one. These are nothing but rationalisations to try and make yourself feel better for not doing something that you should be doing, or want to be doing. But, if you really want success to be yours, you need to stop making excuses and get out there! The other side of the fear of failure is procrastination. Putting things off will only leave them dangling over your head in a big ball of guilt, for you feel bad that you're putting them off. By facing up to what needs to be done and getting on with it, you will give yourself a big sense of relief and freedom, as well as making room for some truly wonderful stuff to come in!

13. Fear of being on our own

Many of us are scared that we'll be abandoned by those we care about, and that we'll end up alone and lonely. Trouble is, this fear can lead to a sense of desperation clouding your vision, and leaving you making the wrong choices about the wrong people.

Things will always turn out the way they're meant to, and being on your own is not the end of the world. You can't be lonely if you like the person you're alone with. Learn to start to love yourself, and to enjoy your own company, and you'll find that the power of that fear dampens down considerably. We should choose to be with others because we want to be, not because we need to be.

14. Comparison

Happiness is not about having what you want, but about wanting what you have. When you compare yourself to those around you, it rarely leaves you feeling good about yourself. And in a world of social media saturation, it's easier to get on the comparison train than ever before. But, you don't know the whole story of what's going on with that person; you're only focusing on the parts you want to see. And, I promise you that there are many people who feel jealous of you when they compare their own lives to yours. Yes, really! There's always someone who'd willingly trade places with you, and it's time to focus on being grateful for the many blessings that you do have in your life. You may not have everything your heart desires, but you do have many reason to be both happy and thankful, if you choose to see them that is.

15. Expectations

How many times have you played a scenario out inside your head? The mini movie projects into the corners of your mind showing you how things are going to go, and what everyone is going to say and do. When you focus on one outcome only, you may see anything else as failure, even if the outcome is better for you. Or, you may miss out on a golden opportunity because you're so focused on the one you have set your sights on. Life doesn't always go to plan, and if we can be open-minded and go with the flow, we open ourselves to all it has to offer for us.

16. The past and the future

It's making things really hard on yourself if your attention is focused on what happened in the past, or the fear of what could happen in the future. By keeping your mind on the yesterdays of your life, or the endless tomorrows, you are robbed of what's happening right now. And that, in turn, can stop you being happy right now! I'm not saying you can't take a nostalgic look at your life, neither am I saying you shouldn't plan for your future. All I am saying is be careful of where the dominance of your attention is focused on. Take the lessons from the past and apply them to your life, now and in the future. Think about where you want your life to go, and what goals you have for your future. But don't forget your life is happening right now! And you don't need to put your happiness off a second longer. You deserve to be happy in every single minute.

Learning to let go is not the easiest task in the whole world. You have been engaged with some of these for your entire life, and it's not going to be a one time, overnight thing of removing them from your life. Some of these form the core values of who you are, even though they're only pulling you down, and it's going to take time to remove them altogether. But every day gives us the chance to start afresh with a clean slate. We can seek to shrug off all that holds us back, and be open to the present moment, knowing that we have the power to create our own happy future for ourselves.

You may know and understand this on a logical level, but actually bringing the concept into your life may prove trickier. Here are some top tips to help you get started:

1. Meditation – You don't have to retreat to a mountaintop and chant to be able to meditate. You can if you really want, but I think this stereotype of what meditation is still puts a lot of people off the idea of even trying. Meditation is stillness, quietness, and connecting to you. And the way to do this is through the breath. By

bringing your focus to the action of inhaling and exhaling, you'll be able to quieten the constant chatter of the mind, which will then make it easier to engage with the other tips on this list. You can never stop your thoughts by the way, but you don't have to give them the same amount of attention that you do normally. As you focus on your breath, you will find that thoughts naturally come back in, and that's okay! That doesn't mean you can't meditate and should give up. Imagine your thoughts as waves on the shore. Let them roll in and roll back out again by themselves, and bring your attention back to your breath. By making room for quietness in your life, even in small amounts, you can gain real clarity of self.

2. Understand the journey – We get emotionally caught up in our own story, and it can be hard to see ourselves without a shedload of judgements and emotional baggage. Try to see your history as an outsider looking in. Hold off judging yourself, and simply be an observer. You are not your past. The situations you have been through and the people you have known along the way have created your experiences, but they didn't create you. By looking at your life as a third party, you can start to see repeated behaviours, and then you can begin to see why you have held on to things which have brought you very little happiness in return. Understanding your journey helps foster a sense of awareness, and this awareness will help you to break the cycle.

3. Accept your history – When you carry around a sense of anger or bitterness towards your past, you're hurting no one but yourself. This emotional baggage becomes a literal wardrobe of pain on your back, burdening you and weighing you down. By accepting your history and the people who have been part of your journey, you can start to let go of this burden and set yourself free. Your circumstances don't define who you are; you define who you are, and you can't change the things that have happened. Fighting them in the belief and hope that you can is a colossal waste of time

and energy.

4. Put the wardrobe down! – Your story – the judgements, ideals, material things – they don't have to be carried around with you like some martyr stick that you continue to beat yourself with. They do not make you a more powerful or better person, and believing that they do can hold you back from moving forward to where you want to be. So too can the expectations of who you're supposed to be, or what you're supposed to be doing. Put your wardrobe down! Let go of all that crap, and make room for the good stuff to come in. You'll find that once you consciously let go of stuff that's not working for you, you'll naturally draw in new opportunities and abundance. They've been waiting to come in, but there's been no room!

5. Who are you really? – Ask yourself the following questions, and answer them as honestly as you can. It's worthwhile grabbing some paper and a pen for this, as you can then refer back to your answers whenever you need to align yourself with them:

- Your core beliefs
- Your life goals
- What are you actively doing to pursue your life goals?

Are your goals aligned with your core beliefs? If not, it may be worth considering the thought that it's time for some new ones – whether that be beliefs, goals or actions! What actions do you need to start doing to align your goals with your beliefs? Consider proactive steps that you can do every day to move yourself where you want to be in alignment with who you truly are.

6. Detach and flow – When we have a fixed idea of what the outcome should look like and how it's going to happen, we can actually miss out on truly wonderful things; even if they come

in a different-shaped box from what we were expecting. We may overlook them or dismiss them completely because they're different from what we were expecting. Detaching from the outcome and flowing with the journey will allow the right opportunities to come to you. Detaching doesn't mean you don't care, it just means that you trust that things will work out as they're supposed to, and you won't stop yourself from receiving all the good stuff that's out there for you (that you haven't even thought of!).

7. Let kindness be your guide – A lot of issues spring up from running over the past, or worrying about the future. You can take yourself out of this mindset by extending kindness to others. Whether it's donating some food to a food bank, opening the door for someone else, or paying for someone else's coffee – making someone else feel better will put your own issues into perspective. Kindness is a wonderful way to come back to the core essence of who you are: love.

8. Keep your belief levels high – You have to believe in your own abilities to be happy, and to achieve what you need in order to make this a reality. Alongside this, you also need to believe that the Universe is infinite; it has abundance to give to all, and is not limited in what it can provide. Neither does it play favourites by giving opportunities to particular people and ignoring others. Everyone has the same access to all the good stuff that's available, and we're all worthy of having it. Believe that you have a divine life purpose, and that the Universe is working with you to make it happen. Believe that holding on to all that no longer serves you does nothing but hold you back and keep you stuck. Keep those belief muscles strong, for they are what's going to keep you moving forward to where you want to be.

9. Don't forget to smile! – Life can be tough enough without getting caught up in serious mode. Letting go of all that stuff that

isn't working for you is supposed to help make your life better; so don't forget to actually smile along the way! You're consciously taking control of your life here, and moving yourself to a positive place. Having fun and bringing some laughter into your day will encourage you to keep letting go of the negative. The more you see yourself enjoying life, the more you'll want to keep moving in that direction more and more.

10. Be a human being – We get so caught up in keeping busy, active, and focusing on tasks that we can forget to actually just stop and take a moment to breathe. We are human beings, not human doings. Be grateful that you are here, and that you get a chance to let go like this. There are many who have gone before you, as well as many who are living their lives right now, who didn't have that same opportunity for so many reasons. You have the power to change your life, and to start to align yourself with being happy; and that is truly an amazing thing. Let go and just be.

Let go of all the junk, and embrace a brighter future.

Happiness is a state of mind

Rejection is Redirection

When I was 17 I had an audition for *Eastenders*. In my head, I built it up to be this golden opportunity. I'd walk in to the audition room, and they'd say, 'YES!' straightaway without me even having to utter a word. They'd be blown away by the sheer presence of me, and would want to cast me straightaway. I'd become the nation's sweetheart overnight, and would be featured in all the magazines and talk shows. Finally, Hollywood would beckon me, and I'd be a film star in no time at all.

In my head I had it all worked out. So much so, that I practically walked in to that audition room on a cloud of pride and arrogance. I had believed my own daydream as being a done deal.

No prizes for guessing I didn't get the part.

At the time, I was distraught. Devastated that the vision that had been so clear within the confines of my mind had dared not come to fruition in real life. I'm sad to say that I became a melodramatic drama queen about the whole thing, and was convinced my life was over.

But it wasn't... obviously, or I wouldn't be writing this book...

What did happen was that I was redirected to something else. And that's the way it's been for every supposed failure in my life. Whether it's the job I didn't get that actually led to a new door of opportunity; the relationship that broke my heart, but which led to new meetings with new people; or the mistakes that I've beaten myself up over, but which have pointed me on to the path of success. Nothing has been an all-out failure, no matter how much I believed it to be just that at the time.

For, everything happens for a reason, and nothing is wasted. Along the way, I have had experience teaching, doing drama, writing, and working with the public. As each thing slipped by the wayside, it was all too easy to think that I'd failed and wasted my time. But now I see that it's all been part of the plan. For now, as a spiritual writer, speaker and teacher, I have all the skills necessary from those experiences to make my work a success. Don't buy into the failure mindset – see it for what it is: signposts all directing you to where you're meant to be.

How do you see yourself? Do you see yourself as you really are, in all your greatness and wonder, or do you have a diluted sense of yourself that keeps you small and lesser? When you see yourself as less than you really are, you don't allow yourself to expand and explore into the furthermost parameters of your potential. You dwell on the lower rung of the ladder, looking up wistfully but not daring to climb. Seeing yourself this way distorts *everything*, including supposed failure. Any kind of mistake or failure is taken as further proof of how rubbish and unworthy you are. In your eyes, you are but a mere speck on the face of existence, and the world becomes a big and scary place that you don't deserve to take up space on.

Think of all the things and people that have threatened to pull you down and stop you in your tracks. At the time, they may have felt like a brick wall reaching up into the Heavens, but you somehow found a way to overcome the obstacles. They didn't stop you, and you're still here. Know that any further failure is simply redirecting you to where you need to be. You have simply been delayed from your successes, not denied them altogether.

Most of us fear rejection and will do anything we can to get the approval we crave. As a consequence of that, we tend to avoid anything we perceive could come with the merest hint of rejection like the plague, but getting a 'No' from someone doesn't necessarily mean they're rejecting you. Indeed, if you have this connection within your mind, you're pretty much guaranteed to get upset every time someone says 'No' to you, because you'll take it personally. Hearing this 'No' doesn't equate with rejection, unless you choose to see it that way. It is possible to see it another way (as redirection to something better), but it has to be a conscious decision to do so.

Another reason for being rejected could be that the person doing the rejecting is in a bad place at that moment in time; their decision is all about them and not actually about you. Your perception has clouded your vision as to how you view the rejection, but it can be tough to see in that moment that their own perception is not exactly crystal clear. So many of us live in our own bubbles, and are overly concerned about how we feel. But actually, not everything is about us, and opening your mind to that can take you out of your Me Bubble. It helps you see that the other person is too wrapped up in their own bubble to make an objective decision right now. Does that mean their rejection is any less painful? No, not necessarily, but it can help you from spiralling down into a pit of self-loathing and misery. Perspective is everything.

I tell you one thing though, rejection can be a good thing. Don't look at me like I've lost the plot! Consider this: not only is it redirecting you to where you're meant to be, but it's also making you stronger in the process. Floating through life on a cloud of *'Yes'* and privilege seems to be a lovely idea, and one a lot of us secretly dream of, but in reality there is a pay-off from that; you don't have the need to find out how strong you are. As the old saying goes – *'What doesn't kill you makes you stronger'*, or as I like to say, *'What doesn't kill me better start running, because I'm getting back up stronger than ever!'*

At the moment of rejection, you won't feel like this, by the by. At that moment, you won't feel like a warrior taking on the world, you'll feel more like a bawling, sobbing mess in the corner. And that's okay! Trust me when I say that there is nothing wrong with crying and letting out your emotions. Indeed, the issues come when we try to push them down and pretend like everything's fine. Cry, shout, hit pillows – just get it out of you; but don't wallow in misery for too long. Let it go and learn from the experience, then move on.

And what is the lesson? Well, maybe the situation is meant for you, but you're not ready to go down the path yet. So, it's not a rejection, but a temporary pause until everything is aligned and ready for you. Of course, you may not necessarily know this at the time, but you have to trust the process and know that you'll be where you're meant to be, at the right time. But there is another consideration… and I'm afraid it's one that you may not want to hear… this situation is not meant for us at all. Ouch, right?

That tunnel vision of keep our focus set on only one thing can be really limiting. We believe that only this one particular thing is the right thing for us, and if it doesn't happen it can literally feel like we've been squashed flat. It is important to set goals in life, and for some goals to matter more than others. Doing this puts you in the proactive mode of making your dreams come true, rather than just simply waiting for them to magically fall in your lap. But when you give too much weight to only one thing, you could be setting yourself up for a fall.

Know that you'll always be where you're meant to be. Look at yourself five years ago – you had not idea that your life would have unrolled the way it has over these last few years, so who's to know what the future has in store for you? To me, that's so exciting, because the possibilities are endless. Yes, rejection can suck big time when it hits you, but if it leads you to happiness, fulfilment and all things sparkly, you'll actually end up glad that you didn't get the thing you cared so much about. Or, if you get rejected and you still have your heart set on that path, then it's worth considering another route. Life doesn't have to unfold in only one way, and you could take the rejection as a big kick up the bum to prove everyone wrong and make it happen! Don't let yourself fall into a pity party for one – it's a miserable idea, and you deserve better.

Don't put all your eggs in one basket (no matter how sparkly it is), and don't let one person determine your happiness.

The happiest people don't have the best of everything, they just make the best of everything

Self-Care is Not Selfish

As I mentioned previously, in 2012 I gave birth to twins. For the first few months after my babies came home, we had weekly visits from a health visitor. She would come to weigh and measure the babies, and see how we were all doing. She was a lovely woman, who didn't just focus on the twins. She knew what I had been through, and was still going through, and was incredibly supportive. You can imagine my shock one week when she told me off!

Katie, will you sit down! Every time I come over, you're making cups of tea, doing the dishes or putting the washing on – what about you, hey? Let me tell you, you can't draw water from an empty well. If you're not looking after yourself, how on Earth are you going to able to look after them?

I had been so busy nurturing everyone else and being a people pleaser that I'd forgotten to look after me! The health visitor's words hit a nerve because I knew she was spot on. Happy mum = happy kids after all. I'd put myself so far at the bottom of my own list that I wasn't even on the page! I knew things had to change, or there was no way I was going to be able to cope with all the stresses that having newborn twins were going to throw at me. Thankfully, her words were the catalyst I needed, and self-care is something I've been working on ever since.

I wonder if this story has struck a chord or two with you. I know I'm not alone in my issues with self-care; so many see it as something that is predominately selfish in nature. Or even as something we might do once we've tackled everything else on our list first. It's as if everyone else's needs are far more important than our own, or even worse we start 'shoulding' all over ourselves. You know the one – *'I should be eating better'*, *'I should be doing more exercise'*. Hardly a recipe for authentic and loving self-care! How are you supposed to nurture yourself if you're approaching it with a lorry load of guilt and fear? Loving self-care is all about caring for ourselves, honouring who we are, nurturing ourselves, and giving ourselves the love we deserve. Doing this not only benefits us, but has a lovely knock-on effect of benefitting everyone around us too. Why? Because:

1. They see that your needs are important, and actually start treating you better – whether it's a conscious decision on their part or not.
2. You inspire them to look at their own self-care practices.
3. You're a happier and nicer person to be around! Sorry to sound like a grumpy puss, but when you're not looking after yourself, you end up resentful and bitter. You secretly want your needs met, but don't vocalise it. So you end up a seething volcano, waiting to explode at any second. The minute you start to look after yourself, the sunshine comes out again!
4. You can't look after anyone if you're not looking after yourself first.

I'm not saying this is something that's easy. Our lives are so full of so many things, that this may seem like another chore to add to your never-ending list. But I don't want you to roll your eyes and sigh at this, for it's not about sticking to a detailed, scheduled plan or keeping up with the neighbours. It's about remembering that you're important too. That you deserve to take care of yourself, and by doing so you can give nourishment to your soul whilst also being more available for the truly important people in your life.

For self-care is not always about engaging in what you feel most like doing, but rather is on what is best for you in that moment. So yes, eating a bar of chocolate bigger than your head, or binge-watching Netflix for hours on end may make you feel good in the short term, but true long-term benefits come from really nurturing and taking care of what your body, mind and spirit needs. Besides, those feelings of stress, anxiety and depression will still be on the other side of instant gratification; in fact, you may have just made them ten times worse by giving in to your base needs. Look, there's nothing wrong with a little indulgence every now and then (I'm as guilty for binge-watching TV as the next person) – it can be really good to relax and treat yourself in this way. But, when this kind of activity becomes the daily norm rather than an occasional treat, you have to consider whether you're truly engaging in real self-care. And like anything that's good for you, self-care can take a lot of work. We all have busy schedules, and it may be tempting to ignore our own needs in favour of another tick on our to-do lists. Self-care isn't about giving in to every small whim your mind presents you with; it's looking after your health, even when you don't necessarily want to.

Bear in mind, too, that one person's self-care cloud 9 is another's idea of Hell on Earth. Self-care is totally subjective, and you shouldn't try to compete with those around you because you are a unique individual. There'll be some whose idea of bliss is to go away on a long weekend camping, hiking and getting back to nature; for others, being put in that environment would be torture. You don't need to give in to your indulgent desires every day, but you do need to ensure that your self-care regime works for you, and is in line with your practicalities, physical abilities, and preferences. Don't force yourself to do something just because it feels like what everyone else is doing on social media!

Your ego may try to convince you that all this self-care is making you like an ostrich – simply burying your head in the sand and hiding from your problems. But self-care actually comes from really knowing yourself, so that you see when something in your life isn't right, it helps you to see what you can do about it. For example, you may be feeling really lost and flat. Your initial go-to is to do things to lift you up. You enrol in dance classes and get connected to your creativity. Whilst you're doing these activities, you do feel happier, but the moment they finish, the weight of greyness crashes down on you again. In that instance, true self-care comes from investigating the problem further, and seeing what's at the root of the problem. You may even benefit from talking to a counsellor to help you work it out. Using self-care to just give you a quick fix of happiness in the present isn't great for you in the long run either. It's better for you to address any issues that are holding you back from your happiness, so you can be free.

One of the core beliefs that's passed down to us is that it's a good thing to look after others, and to put their needs before our own. With this belief self-care may seem like the most selfish and self-centred thing in the world. If we're supposed to put everything we can into caring and nurturing others, how can looking after our own needs be a good thing? But, just because you feel selfish, doesn't make it true. Your inner jerk is not screaming at you because you are one; it's simply flagging up for you because your actions go against years of being told that you have to behave in a certain way.

But if you always put others before yourself, where and when do you stop? There are literally millions of people in the world who need love and help. You could spend every waking hour of your life looking to put others before yourself, and you'd barely scratch the surface. This isn't to make you feel bad by the way, neither should that knowledge stop you from helping people, but there has to be an element of balance in all you do. Why are you so unimportant? What makes your needs less important than everyone else's?

If you don't practise self-care, you're like a car running on empty. You may try to keep moving forward, but you aren't going to get very far. When you're constantly living your life on empty, you don't have the energy to help **anyone**; not you or anyone else for that matter. If you can't take care of yourself, then you will need to start looking to others to help you. This, in turn, will then foster feelings of resentment and guilt – hardly the stuff of happiness!

Consider this too: without self-care, how are you supposed to know who you are or want you really want? Your intuition and feelings are constantly giving you signs as to what's best for you in every moment. When you fail to look after yourself, it's like walking around with your fingers permanently lodged in your ears against yourself! Your intuition is your Higher Self/Spirit/ guides/angels talking to you, and leading you to your highest good. This soft voice is loving and nurturing, but it's important to make the time to listen and act upon its guidance. It's not like a magical fairy godmother that'll make all your wishes come true without you having to do much. Yes, it'll guide you to where you need to be, but without you following through, its voice will fade into the background until you can't hear it so well anymore. Like any part of your being, the more you use it, the stronger it gets. Self-care is an invaluable way to develop the connection to your inner guidance, because it becomes like a dialogue between you and your inner best friend.

Besides anything else, regular self-care allows you to take better care of others. Airlines guide parents to put their own oxygen mask on in an accident before they put on their child's. Why? Because you'll be in no fit state to help anyone when you haven't got the capacity to do so! Self-care gives you more health, compassion, and energy. All of them mean you can then help more people for longer; the thing that most of us are taught to do anyway!

Now that you know why self-care is so essential, what kinds of things does it entail? Well, there are lots of ways to look after yourself:

- Drinking enough water.
- Ensuring lots of fresh air.
- Exercise – move your body in some way every single day. It doesn't have to be a formal sport – climbing the stairs, walking and housework all count too!
- Healthy diet – aim for 5–7 portions of fruits and vegetables

every day to get all the nutrients your body needs to be healthy.

- Get enough sleep – your body recovers and repairs itself whilst you sleep, so it can really affect your whole body and mind if you aren't getting enough. Every person needs a different amount of sleep, but it's typically around 7–8 hours. It's so important to ensure you're getting sufficient sleep, so do what you need to in order to help facilitate this.
- Try to adopt a positive attitude as much as you can, and surround yourself with people who do the same. It's damn near impossible to be a Little Miss or Mr Sunshine in every second of every day, but holding on to the intention of being positive right down in your core means it's something that you'll always come back to. Don't forget you're also hugely likely to take on the beliefs and traits of the five main people in your life… so make sure they're not bringing you down. Sometimes we need to say 'goodbye' to certain people for our own self-care. Not everyone is going to stay in your life forever, and letting them go can be the best thing you ever did.
- Find an interest that's outside of your home and family life. For a long time I felt just like the wife and the mum. There's nothing wrong with being these things, but it's equally important to maintain your own individuality. Spending some time doing the things that you enjoy every week just for you will help to maintain your own identity.
- Don't be afraid to be on you own. You can't be lonely if you like the person you're alone with. Grabbing some me time where you can is vital for your emotional and mental health. Even if it means locking the bathroom door for half an hour – do it! The peace that comes from that space will allow you to gather your thoughts and come back to centre.
- Ask for help. Look, I'm sorry to burst your bubble, but you don't actually have a giant S on your chest and a

cape on your back. You may feel as though you have to do everything by yourself and save the world, but you really don't. At some point in all of our lives there comes a time when we struggle and feel as though it all gets a bit too much. Are you going to carry on struggling like the overburdened martyr you are, or are you going to ask for help? Letting others help you is not a sign of weakness; it's a huge sign of strength! It shows that you know your physical, emotional and mental boundaries, and you're not going to push yourself past the breaking point for some silly notions of pride or martyrdom. Besides, people like it when you ask them for help! It makes them feel useful and needed. So ask away and make your life that little bit easier.

There will always be demands and stresses put on you – that's just the way life is I'm afraid. I can't magic them away with a sprinkle of pixie dust, but I can help you see how important it is to look after yourself. See yourself as a sparkly bucket (go with me on this). Stress seeks to put holes in the bottom and drain your happiness away. If you don't keep topping the bucket up, you're going to run out pretty quickly. Self-care is putting happy sand into your bucket. It means the pressures of life are not going to drain you to such a point that you feel as though you're running on empty and have nothing left to give. So keep looking after yourself and shovelling the sand in; you can't get better self-care than that!

Make today so awesome that yesterday gets jealous

Money is Magic

What's the one thing in life that causes the most stress, worries and obsessive behaviour? No, not relationships, although they certainly can fall into that territory! I'm talking about one of the main focuses of all our lives: money.

Money. So much of our lives is spent wanting it, needing it, earning it, spending it and then regretting what we did with it.

Love it, hate it, or indifferent, it plays a massive part in all of our lives, whether we want it to or not. And, most people wouldn't necessarily equate it with happiness... not unless we won the lottery anyway!

That's the thing, isn't it? We all have this magic number in our heads; a figure where we believe we could be happy, and everyone's number is different. Whether it's £100,000, a million, or a hundred million, we all have this dream that we'd win or be given a huge sum of money and all of our worries would fade away. That we could be happy and really start living our lives.

That's why an estimated 70% of the UK population (that's 45 million people) regularly play the National Lottery every week since its launch in 1994. We have a belief that if we won, we'd be able to quit our jobs and live a life of luxury and happiness. But does winning these huge sums of money really solve everything? There are plenty of winners who have had their dreams come true and been able to do things that they couldn't have otherwise afforded. I'm not here to paint the National Lottery in a bad way at all. It has been a miraculous thing for many people, but it isn't the answered prayer that everyone seems to think it is. Like the 16-year-old who won £1.9 million in 2003. She has since said that winning the Lottery was 'a curse' and it drove her to consider taking her own life. She has since found happiness, but it's not come from money. She says she only has £2,000 left of her original winnings, but it's through finding love and direction in her life that she's now truly happy.

And that's the key, isn't it?

Yes, having money can be a truly wonderful thing. It takes away the worry and stress of wondering how you're going to pay your bills, and look after your family, absolutely. For those who are struggling financially, having money will make them happier, because it eases off the constant pressure of worrying about it. But it doesn't necessarily equal happiness in the long run. Why? Because it doesn't change the core of who you are. If you were a lost and unhappy person before you came into lots of money, suddenly getting it isn't going to change things; you'll still be that same person inside. It's like trying to run away from all your problems – it doesn't work because you take you with you wherever you go! Money makes life easier, but true happiness comes from within you; it's a real inside job.

We all have basic needs, and we all deserve to be happy. I'm definitely not recommending that you live a life of a poor recluse to get your happy groove on; far from it! You do deserve abundance, to have nice things, and to live a life that doesn't revolve around the stress of financial worries; we all do. All I am saying is that deferring your happiness until you reach the magical number in your head, where you get the monetary figure you've been dreaming of, is sheer nonsense. As we saw in the chapter *The Time is Now*, putting your happiness off to a magical future destination is dangerous. That time may never come, and it's robbing you of living your life right now. How can you really enjoy each wonderful moment of your life if you're continuously obsessing over the future? You have no idea what next week will bring, let alone five years down the line! But your life is happening right now. Don't miss it worrying about tomorrow, for when these moments are gone, no amount of money can ever get them back.

Our relationship is determined by so many things: our upbringing, education, employment, and our own psychological factors. There's no getting around it – if our relationship with money was a Facebook status, it would be down as *it's complicated*.

Having a sudden influx doesn't necessarily mean you're going to be happier; although there's a correlation between what you spend your money on and how happy you are. Money gives you a greater sense of freedom in your life, so you're not tied down to the daily slog and grind of a monotonous life. If having an extra income means you can now afford to work less, or afford quality childcare, then this is going to give you the chance to experience a life of less stress that may not have been open to you before.

You may imagine that having loads of money means you can now buy all the things you've been dreaming of but not been able to get. The big house, the cars, the exotic holidays and the technology; all the things that come with a hefty price ticket. What's interesting to note, however, is that things don't necessarily equal being happy. Yes, in the short term, having the latest widescreen, HD, 3D, all-singing, all-dancing TV may give you an initial buzz of excitement, but the novelty soon wears off. Within a few months it becomes just another piece of furniture, and you'd be looking for the next thing to give you that same feeling you had before. Don't get me wrong, if someone offered to buy me this high-tech gadget, I'm not exactly going to rush to say, 'No,' but I know that getting it is not going to make me happier long term.

Actually it's experiences that lead to happiness, not things. Why? Because they lead to lovely memories that you can reminisce over for months, or even years to come; each memory bringing another sparkly burst of happiness to mind. You also get the delicious anticipation that comes beforehand, which can feel like a kid waiting for Santa to come. We imagine ourselves in the experience, and share the details with others. The whole experience of having that time can be a pleasure from start to finish. Even when it doesn't go to plan! Don't frown at me, it's true. Let's say you go away on a camping trip. You've planned every detail, bought all the equipment, and you're really looking forward to it. But your trip has one teeny tiny flaw: you're going camping in the UK. I'm a huge fan of my country, but it doesn't exactly have the best weather... Before you know it, your entire week's camping adventure is a washout, and you feel like you've been on a water rapids ride at a theme park rather than a relaxing getaway. During the experience itself, it may be sheer misery, but something magical happens on the drive home: hindsight kicks in. What was the trip from Hell suddenly becomes the funniest story in the world that you can share with others! From the tent sliding down the hill in a deluge of rainwater, to your sleeping bag feeling more like a paddling pool – the storytelling aspect of the experience brings happiness as you share it with others. It would seem joy can spring up from the most unlikely sources!

There's another aspect of money that can lead to happiness: using it to help others. Whether it's giving money to charity, or helping a friend in need – there's a real sense of well-being that comes from giving. I spoke about this in the chapter *Use Your Kindness Blaster 3000*, but there is a real sense of happiness that comes from being kind. By ensuring that the kindness you give comes from love without expecting anything in return, and that it's something that can really empower the recipient, you will help to ensure that it's an amazing gift that benefits you both. Not only will they feel grateful and unbelievably happy, you will feel a warmth in your soul like nothing else.

What if money isn't exactly flowing your way, however? What if you don't even have a bucket to pee in, and the very notion of buying experiences and giving money away seems nothing better than some magical dream? In that case, it can be hard to try and create a good relationship with all things money-orientated – it becomes all consuming. The desperate and overwhelming concern that plagues every day of your life, and keeps you awake at night. How can you seek to turn things around for yourself?

Money matters have their roots in how your parents dealt with their finances. Our core beliefs are formed by the age of five, and your childhood is spent with your parents on some untouchable pedestal. Indeed, it's not until you get older and get out into the big wide world that you realise that not everyone's families are like yours; you think it's the norm. So, if one or both of your parents had an unhealthy relationship with money, it's highly likely that you will too. For we tend to repeat behaviours unless we make a conscious effort to change them. Maybe they always lived hand to mouth and you never knew if there'd be a red letter through the letterbox or enough food in the fridge. The concept of savings was an alien idea; money was like water through their fingers, and there was never enough. Or, maybe your parents were tighter than a whale in a shoebox. They never liked to spend out on anything, there were never any nice treats or exciting days out, and everything was second-hand. Money was something you clung to out of the fear that it may run out and you'd never be able to replace it.

Regardless of your beliefs about money, it can have a real knock-on effect on how you perceive your finances. To truly understand this, it's really important to take an honest look at yourself and see how you feel about money. Does the idea of people talking about anything financial make you want to stick your fingers in your ears and go, 'La-la-la-la!'? Or, is there never enough month at the end of your money? This honest self-reflection shouldn't come with a shedload of negativity and criticism by the way; that isn't going to help anyone. Simply observe your attitudes, feelings and beliefs about money and write them down so you have them to refer back to. Once you've established what's going on for you, then you can seek to change it for the better.

If you are someone who spends before they have it and never seems to have enough, there is an answer to your issues... but it might not make you jump for joy I'm afraid. It's time to get responsible about the whole shebang, and dare I say it, grow up. A lot of financial issues comes from a certain level of immaturity around the topic. Saving premiums, ISAs, mortgages, stocks – it can all seem as enticing as watching paint dry. But, if you're going to develop a healthier relationship with money then you need to educate yourself about these things, and don't be so afraid of them all. Sit and write down all of your incomings and outgoings, and see what's what. What bills go out, when and how much is each one? Are there any shortcomings in your budget that you might need to look at? By getting yourself fully informed on what the reality is in your money life, you can start to take control of it. This may not sound like the happiest homework I can give you, but a lack of control will only give you stress, anxiety, sleepless nights and difficult times. Happiness is not all sunshine and rainbows you know, it's ensuring there are no stresses in any area of your life and, if there are, doing something about it. Remember, you are the captain of your own ship!

If, on the other hand, the mere thought of spending money makes you come out in a cold sweat, it's time to consider loosening the purse strings a bit. Look, I know it's not going to be easy, but life is short and precious, and you can't take your money with you when you go! No one lay on their deathbed and wished they'd put more money in the bank. They wished they'd appreciated every magical moment of their life, and experienced all the wondrous things it has to offer. Besides, the Universe works on the premise of give and take; a perfect balance that keeps everything ticking over nicely. If you keep taking and never give anything back, you are putting yourself out of balance, and this in turn could block you from receiving all the good stuff that life has to offer. Add the fact that you deserve reward for the work you do, and you can hopefully see that spending money isn't necessarily the worst thing in the world. I'm not saying that you should go mad and throw all your salary at the altar of consumerism every month, but it's okay to spend *some* money. You won't be splashed across the front covers of every daily newspaper, or anything as scandalous as that; but you will gain back some healthy balance in your finances and your life.

Start small. On payday, treat yourself to one small item you've had your eye on. A lipstick maybe, or a book. Watch your inner child dance with glee at this treat! The world won't fall around your ears, but you will feel better about yourself; less resentful about all the work you do. As time goes on, you may feel more comfortable with letting go of those purse strings a bit more, but don't rush yourself. This, like everything, is a work in progress. It's the committed dedication to keep bringing more happiness into your life, and the knowledge that you deserve this. You deserve it all!

Money doesn't make the world go round (though I'm sure there are people in governments and big corporations that would disagree with me); love does. But money is the mode by which we operate in modern society. It does play a big part in all of our lives, whether we like it or not. And, although it may not seem like the basis of happiness, it's important to understand the role it plays in your life. Having an unhealthy relationship with money leads to true unhappiness, through stress, fear and anxiety. Trying to create a healthier relationship with your finances places you back in control, and thus helps you to be happier in the long run.

Be happy
Be bright
Be you

All You Need is Love (and Maybe a Cookie or Two)

Ah, love.

Forget money (not completely, as we've seen that can lead to a whole heap of problems), it's love that's the main focus of all of our lives.

Most of us spend a hell of a lot of time thinking about it, chasing it, worrying about it, and talking about it. Thousands of songs have been written about love. It's the theme of countless books, films, poems and plays. It's inspired the great, and toppled the rest of us. Love is… everything.

My own relationship with love has been interesting to say the least. Although I started out well with my first proper boyfriend from the ages of 16 to 18. Kind, romantic and loving, I couldn't believe my luck that I started off so well. Shame I wasn't able to replicate this kind of love in the relationships I had after that first one. Time and time again I ended up in relationships that weren't great. A veritable plethora of control, domineering, manipulation, aggression and poor treatment. Every time the relationship ended, I vowed that the next one would be different, and I dreamed of my knight in shining armour who would whisk me away in a cloud of love and romance. And yet, sure enough, the next one would start and I'd be surprised that I'd ended up with a man who was pretty much the same as the one who had gone before. Why was love such a struggle for me, when it was the one thing that I really wanted?

It took me a LONG time to figure out why I kept repeating this behaviour. Seriously, I won't tell you how long it was; you'll only talk about me! But one day it hit me like a ten-tonne truck: I was attracting bad relationships because I had a bad relationship with myself.

Drop the mic.

As Oprah herself would say, *'That was an aha moment!'*

And it really was! It changed the game, because I saw my part in the whole sorry saga. Hell, I saw that I was the literal epicentre of my experience of love. I was drawing partners to me that mirrored how I felt about myself and, because my self-worth and self-esteem were lower than a worm's belly after an all-you-can-eat buffet at Soils R Us, I was putting myself in relationships with men who just aligned themselves with my own beliefs. And I tended to accept their crappy behaviour because I didn't believe I deserved any better. Talk about a recipe for unhappiness and melodrama!

How we feel about ourselves has a mahoosive part to play in our relationships, and yet most of us don't even tend to think about the relationship we have with ourselves or how important that is. How is anyone supposed to love you deeply, wholly and completely if you can't love yourself? You'll create a wall so big around your heart that no one will be able to scale it fully, even when you keep asking the Universe to bring you your soulmate and one true love. Even a fairy-tale prince wouldn't be able to love you in the way you need if you can't love yourself first; it has to start with you!

Love takes many forms in our lives. We naturally jump to love in the romantic sense in our heads, but that's not all it encompasses. Love for our parents, our siblings, grandparents, uncles, aunties, cousins, children, friends, colleagues, and pets. That's a lot of love going around! And each one of those relationships will help to create the person you are, and give you different things at different times. At its purest form, love helps us in so many ways:

- Love leads to better self-esteem.
- Love is a great reliever of stress. It counteracts the fight or flight response that's innately built into us all, and which shows itself when we feel under threat. When the body is under even low levels of stress, it produces a hormone called cortisol. This has been linked to giving a higher risk

of developing such things as diabetes, heart disease and depression. In contrast, love releases the hormone oxytocin, which is the feel-good hormone. This hormone improves your immune system and reduces cardiovascular stress. Love is the sweetest medicine!

- Love improves your mental well-being.
- Have a more positive mood overall.
- Longer life span.
- Better mental and emotional health.

It would seem that love, in whatever form it comes in, truly is good for you in so many ways. But, does love make you happy? The natural and almost automatic response is to say 'yes' – after all, the word 'love' conjures up images of connection, compassion and togetherness. Our society has paired really positive words, images and cultural rhetoric around love that we jump to these without stopping to fully consider our answer. Without pausing to see if these links are true to our own experiences.

Love can certainly make you feel great, of that there is no doubt. But, it isn't all hearts and flowers, sadly. Love can bring a whole heap of misery into your life too, and not just through rows and breakups. Love is associated with the emotions of happiness and joy, but it also has ties to depression and anxiety too. This is because love is not a simple black and white thing of just good feelings, it's also the absence of negative ones.

Why is this? It is all dependent on how much attention we are giving to it. When you are floundering around in the depths of uncertainty, it naturally equates that love is **all you can think about**. We all know those feelings far too well:

Do they love me?
Do they even like me?
Why haven't they called me?
What's he thinking about?

Have I upset her?
Will their friends like me?
Where is this going?

On and on; you can damn near drive yourself crazy! The constant uncertainty that is a natural reaction to love is a recipe for helping you experience both positive and negative emotions. Yes, love can be the most amazing, life altering and firework-feeling situation you will ever experience. But, if you really care about your happiness (and I'm guessing you do, or you wouldn't be reading this book), then you need to be realistic about the fact that love doesn't automatically lead to happiness.

Being happy does affect your success rate in love, however! Happiness is a massively attractive quality, and instantly makes you look like the best version of yourself. How can you not look beautiful/handsome when you're beaming from the inside out? You end up like living, breathing sunshine! Happiness also means that you're more likely to have a longer lasting love with someone too. Let's be honest here: those grey misery misers are hardly going to be your first choice now, are they? The best feature about you is your smile, and everyone looks better when they're happy. So, set your facial muscles to the smile position, and let love come to you!

Relationships can also be our greatest teachers too. Not only are relationships a source of comfort, support, fun and companionship, but they offer major opportunities for personal growth. There are some lessons that cannot be learned outside of a relationship. Every interaction you have ever had will have brought out different sides of you and given you a chance to observe your reactions from a variety of different perspectives. Sometimes it can be unbelievably rough and painful, but their actions, ultimately, unveil a truth and will inspire you take steps towards healing yourself. This is because these connections can trigger you and push your buttons. They are like floor-to-ceiling mirrors placed right in front of us, helping us to witness all those ugly parts of ourselves that we've been avoiding. We hide them from our own awareness, but relationships bring them right out for us to face and deal with. You could say that every person that we meet is serving a higher purpose of furthering our soul's knowledge in the greatest school of them all (i.e. life), and we attract only those who are relevant to each part of our journey.

Having the right people around you who can guide and support you can really help you to live up to your true potential. It doesn't matter if that person is a boss, a teacher, a family member, or a coach – having an individual who inspires and empowers you to be the best you can possibly be is going to help you become truly happy within yourself. But, having an unhealthy relationship is a great teacher for finding your boundaries and self-care. These lessons may not come as quick or be as pleasant to experience (and, believe me, I know what I'm talking about), but you come to see there are those who deserve your time and energies... and those who don't deserve even a second. You deserve to have relationships in your life that only see you receive a certain level of respect and dignity; anything less than that is a waste of everyone's time.

I want to point out something. It's a thing I've noticed over the years in others that has caused big problems in love, but isn't something that people are necessarily aware of. What is it? You can't rely on one person to give you all the love you need. I know what it's like – when you first fall in love, you want to be with them 24/7, and the idea of not being with them is so unthinkable it actually hurts you. I'm not saying that you should have a polygamous relationship (which means more than one partner. If that's your bag though, go for it! I've never been one to judge!). All I am saying is that there are other people in your life who love you: family, friends. To put all your eggs in one basket is risky. We are complex and multifaceted individuals. We have a wide range of needs, beliefs and interests. The idea that one person out of 7 billion is going to tick all your boxes is insane. Plus, it's an awful lot of pressure on them! By spreading love out to all, you'll find that you end up more satisfied overall. Don't be selfish or greedy with your love; give it away to all those you care about.

Love, as we all know, is the most powerful force in the universe and certainly is a must ingredient if we want to live a happy life.

Buddhism, Christianity, Judaism, Islam, Yoga, Hinduism, and independent thinkers and mystics all around the world have all said the same thing:

They all say that love is the WAY.

But this isn't the typical image of romantic love we think of when we hear the word love. That kind of love can be based on possession and reaching to fill ourselves up so we can feel whole again. This is, ultimately, a pursuit of the ego. This type of love isn't love at all; although we certainly feel like it is.

True love is boundless and universal. It's a state of being which doesn't distinguish or discriminate between white and black, us and them, or even you and me. True love means we realise these boundaries were imaginary constructs in our mind. In many ways, love is a state of being, the very essence of life. Love is the energy we feel when we come in contact with things in a very deep and real kind of way. So, love is the answer. The way to realising this great interconnected nature, as well as seeing the fact that we are whole in spiritual truth, and no longer needing to strive to acquire or accomplish.

How do we find this true love? Well, there's a great practice I do when I'm feeling disconnected, and I want to share it with you so it can help you too. This is to see the light that's within everyone. No matter who it is you're looking at, imagine a bright white light within them. It may be a huge and bright light that is the same size as their body, or something smaller that may be centred on their heart. No matter how you see it, look for this light. Now, I'm not going to lie to you – with some people, this is going to be really easy. The people who are loving, kind and compassionate – you can see their light most of the time anyway. But, what about those individuals who are more, well… a pain in the butt?

Not everyone in the world is as nice and sparkly as you or I, sadly. You will meet people in life who users, abusers and generally not very lovely people. Basically, they have so many issues, they practically wrote the book on it. Does that mean they don't have a light inside of them? There will be those who say it does, but I disagree. We all have our own light; after all, we are spiritual beings having a human experience. It's just that their light is buried beneath layers of fear. It's there, but it's going to take a bit (or even a lot) more effort to see it.

But, when you see the light that's within everyone, you understand that, beneath all the fear and worldly issues, we are all ultimately connected. We are all one. We all want love. We all want to be happy. Seeing this light inside everyone helps you to fully understand what true love is, and to start to extend it to others. Give it a try! It has definitely been an invaluable practice for me.

Let me ask you another question: who is the most important person to love in the whole world? Your parents perhaps? Your children? Your partner? All these are incredibly important, and they all deserve your love by the tanker load, but they aren't the right answer. The person you should love the most is… (drum roll please)… YOU!

Yes, really! Put your cynical eyebrow down, and let me explain.

Loving yourself is the most important relationship you will ever have, because it sets the foundations for every other love in your life. You can't truly love others until you love yourself, or let others love you. When you don't love (or even like) yourself, you set up a blockade bigger than the Great Wall of China to fully develop love for all. Self-love isn't easy. It isn't just a case of creating a meme or putting it in your bio on social media; it takes real courage. You are facing yourself with honesty and seeing yourself exactly as you are, with all the attitudes, biases and perceptions that you have built up since childhood.

So many seek love from others as a way of giving validation to who they are. It's as if they don't feel whole unless someone else makes them feel this way. But, looking for this external validation is a risky strategy. Nothing lasts forever. What if this relationship ends? Does that mean you're suddenly not worthy or important anymore? True validation is a gift you give to yourself, by loving and accepting yourself just as you are. In that sense, it doesn't matter as much who comes and goes in your life; you will never lose sight of how amazing you are.

So, how do we start loving ourselves?

- Know that you deserve to be happy. Happiness is your birthright. You deserve it because you were born to be happy. You don't have to have a certain amount of money, have success, or look a certain way to be worthy; we all are, just as we are.
- Accept yourself as you are. So many of you don't like the way you look, and that makes the process of loving yourself harder. If you are able to change things for the better then take control. Whether it's a healthy diet or exercising more – you have the power to feel better about yourself. If it's something you can't change, then perspective is key. Yes, there are things that may not be to your liking, but I promise you that there are people worse off than yourself. Put your hand on your chest – do you feel your heart beating? Then you're alive, and that is the most amazing thing! You still have the power to be happy and make your life something incredibly special, for you.
- Get your gratitude groove on. Be thankful for the things you like about yourself. Focus on them and send them some love. While you're at it, send some love to your less than yummy parts too; all of you deserves to be loved, not just the sparkly bits.

- Pay attention to what you say and think about yourself. *'I'm not good enough.' 'I'm incompetent.' 'It's all my fault.'* Sound familiar? Would you talk to your best friend in that way? Then why on Earth do you think it's okay to talk to yourself like that? You are a wonderful work in progress. You will make mistakes, and you're not perfect. But, guess what? Every single person who walks this big, beautiful planet is exactly the same! Stop mentally beating yourself up and being so hard on yourself – you're doing great.

- Make time for the things that make your heart sing with joy. Life is extremely busy, and we all have commitments, but it's really important that we make time for ourselves and do things that make us feel good. Saying you don't have time is an excuse; and a lame one at that. I know you procrastinate and waste time doing things that don't necessarily make you any happier (social media scrolling and TV watching anyone?). If you can find time for them, you can definitely make time to do something that makes you happy! Plus, it means that your obligations will be done with less effort, because you'll feel mentally better about doing them.

- Surround yourself with people who really love and appreciate you. This does mean removing people from your life who are toxic, and this can be tough. But, loving yourself means you understand that you deserve to be treated better, and actually doing something about that! There are people who love you for the person you are, not who they want you to be. Bring these people into your life more, and watch your confidence shoot up to the stars!

- Don't be so hard on yourself. Even when you make mistakes... **especially** when you make mistakes! *'Anyone who has never made a mistake has never tried anything new,'* ~ Albert Einstein. If one of the wheels on your car got a flat tyre, would you never drive again? Of course not! You'd change the tyre and get on with your life. Don't throw in the towel when setbacks happen; it's part of life! It doesn't make you a failure or a bad person, so stop putting yourself down. You're doing a whole lot better than you think you are.

- Forgive yourself. Unless you've got a time machine (and you kept that flipping quiet!), you can't change the past. No matter how crappy, embarrassing or downright horrible, it's done and gone. The only thing you can do is learn from it and use those lessons as you move forward. So, let it go and forgive yourself. You'll feel as though a weight the size of ten elephants in ten double-decker buses has been lifted off your shoulders.

- Forgive others. People aren't always the lovely, happy people we want them to be. Sometimes people do things that are hurtful and really damaging; I know that. But, by carrying that pain around with you 24/7, they still have power over you. They are literally robbing you of your happiness, and leaving you with the poison of anger in your heart. Forgiveness doesn't mean you're saying that what they did is okay, and it doesn't mean you have to see or talk to them ever again. This is about you, not them. Forgive them because you deserve peace; you deserve to be happy again.

- Don't compare. You are a unique and miraculous individual. Words cannot begin to do justice to how truly wonderful you are. So, please, stop measuring yourself against other people! They can inspire you to greatness, yes, but don't lose sight of your own specialness. What works out for someone else won't necessarily work for you, and you have to do things in your own fabulous way.

- Stop striving for perfection. I hate to burst your bubble, but you're never going to be 100% perfect – get off that control train right now. There's no such thing as perfect, and you're just setting yourself up for a lifetime of disappointment and stress. Just be you, be happy, and keep doing the best you can. Don't give importance to what others think of you; you are the one that truly counts in your life.

- Don't let anyone make you feel bad about yourself. No one! Loving yourself means you won't allow anyone to treat you badly or make you feel inferior in any way. You understand that you deserve better, and you won't stand for anything less than that. Tell them with love and politeness that you're not happy with how they're treating you. If their behaviour continues, walk away from them as fast as your legs can carry you.
- Treat your body like the temple it is. You only have one body, and it spends its whole time loving, protecting and supporting you. Help your body by nourishing it and giving it some much-needed love. You'll feel better mentally, emotionally and physically.

The number one thing you can do to love yourself?

Believe in you!

If you don't, you're basically carrying around a big sign on your neck that says, 'I'm crap.' No one else will believe in you either, and you'll stop yourself from living the happy life you deserve to have.

Believing in yourself stems from good self-esteem. The word 'esteem' itself means *'to estimate'* in Latin. It can therefore be seen that self-esteem is how we see ourselves. I tell you what though, I haven't ever seen a baby with low self-esteem! We all start off full of love and innocence, and anything that's layered over that is built up over years of being told we're this and that from other people. That's not to say kids themselves are all sweetness and light (as any parent will tell you). The experiences we have during our childhood have a major part to play on how we perceive ourselves. This continues into adulthood and every moment of our lives by the interactions we have with others. Whether they are your parents, friends, partners, colleagues, or little old Mavis who works at the corner shop; every single person will have their impact on your self-esteem, and consequently how much you're then able to believe in yourself. But building up your image of yourself solely on what others think of you – it can prove to be highly destructive for you in many ways.

Self-esteem can be seen as whether you have a certain level of confidence in your worth; your right to be both successful and happy. You know that you cope with any challenges that life throws at you, and you deserve all the wonderful things that your journey has to offer you. When your self-esteem is low over great periods of time, it can have a massively negative impact on the state of your life on a daily basis.

Your self-esteem needs to spring up from how you see yourself. These are your own opinions, not based on the influence of others, or allowing them to tell you what to think. Cultivating a healthy self-esteem is hugely important because it plays a significant role in your determination, energy levels, and vitality. So, let me ask you:

- Do you like yourself?
- Do you think you deserve to be happy?
- Do you think you're a good person?
- Do you deserve to be loved?
- Do you really feel, deep down in your soul, that you are a decent person?

If you say 'no' or struggle to answer these questions, it's time to look at raising your self-esteem angel. Thankfully, there are things you can do to help yourself with this. The first thing is to make positive affirmations your new best friend – they can transform the way you think about yourself, and will thus improve your self-esteem overall. It's changing the way you talk to yourself, because the negative ego can be both persistent and really loud; I swear that girl has a megaphone or something! Many people initially struggle with the idea of affirmations when they first hear of them, because their ego is blowing big fat raspberries at them. It'll tell you that you can't say them because they're not true. How can you tell yourself that you're amazing when you're not? You'll never shut your ego up completely because it's part of you, but it doesn't mean it has to be the actor, writer, director and producer of your life! Take back control, even if you have to fake it until you make it. Here are some examples for you to start working with in your own life:

- I deserve to be happy and successful in every area of my life
- I have power over my own life and the choices I make
- I love and respect myself
- I am an amazing person
- My thoughts and opinions matter
- I know I can achieve anything I set my mind to
- I have something special to offer the world
- I am a unique and special individual
- I feel great about myself and my life

If reading these makes you feel uncomfortable, then that shows you need to read them more! Out loud to yourself in the mirror at least once a day, every single day. New habits take at least 90 days to come into full effect, so this no quick fix. But, if you make the commitment to yourself to keep giving yourself the love you need over and over again, your self-esteem will start to improve dramatically. And that will pave the way for huge doses of both believing in and loving yourself.

While we're on that note, if you really want to start being your own best friend and loving yourself, then you need to practise self-care on a daily basis too. This means you need to ensure you get enough sleep, make sure you're getting enough fluid intake (and no, that doesn't mean alcohol, sorry!), get regular exercise, and eat a balanced diet. A healthy mind is wholly dependent on a healthy body, and looking after yourself is vital for truly loving yourself as you deserve to.

Love is one of the most beautiful and powerful energies in the Universe. It truly does make the world go round. Loving ourselves and spreading love out to everyone will help heal us all.

When it rains
look for
rainbows, when
it's dark look
for stars

Your Purpose is Not Rocket Science...
Unless You're a Rocket Scientist

When I was 16, I had an appointment with a careers advisor at school. I'm sure she was a lovely woman, but I got the distinct impression that she had a tick list and a mission to get all of us on the next part of our journey. As I sat down opposite her, she looked up over her glasses with an expectant air:

'So, what career field do you want to go into once you've left school?'

'I... don't know...' I mumbled, my gaze dropping to my lap.

The woman looked both shocked and annoyed, as though my lack of direction was a personal slight against her and her work. *'You don't know! What do you mean, you don't know?'*

My cheeks burned in shame, but my mouth sealed itself shut tight. All I wanted to do was to get out of that tiny, stuffy room as fast as my legs could carry me.

Taking a deep breath (to calm herself down, I guessed), she huffed, *'Well, have you done anything outside of school: hobbies, part-time jobs, that kind of thing.'*

Ever the people pleaser, I offered her an olive branch to cling to in the storm, *'I've just worked for my mum's friend over the summer. She has her own nursery, you see.'*

Instantly, the career advisor's face brightened, as though someone had switched on the light. *'There you are then! I'll put you down to do a childcare course at college. You'll love it! Off you go back to class then!'*

And that was that. In the space of less than five minutes I felt as though my whole future had been decided for me (mind, asking a 16-year-old what they want to do for the rest of their life is ridiculous; you don't even really know who you are at that point). And that was how I ended up doing a course for two years that I didn't really like, and which I passed by the skin of my teeth. Hardly a golden tale of passion and purpose you might think.

But then, I've had more jobs between the ages of 16 and 30 than you've had changes of underwear. These are some of the jobs I've had:

- Shop assistant
- Nursery nurse
- Barmaid
- English teacher
- Supply teacher
- Preschool supervisor
- Administrator
- Secretary
- Cold caller (not my proudest role, but needs must)
- Housekeeper

My mum likes to say that I have many strings to my bow, but honestly, I had no real clue what I wanted to be or why I was here. And I know I'm not alone. Millions of people all over the world seemingly know that there's a purpose for their life; the reason they are here and meant to be rocking their passion. But, for the life of them, they can't figure out what that 'thing' is. And that's **really** stressful! For those who aren't working in a job that focuses on their passions, that makes them feel fulfilled, and from which they can earn money – this is the dream. And, if you haven't found it yet, you may feel a terrible sense of panic and urgency that your time is running out to find it and get on with it! Arrrrgggghhhhh!

Breathe.

Calm down.

It's not as awful as you may think.

See, the issue stems from the fact that you're led to believe that there's only one thing that you're meant to be doing. That your life purpose is a singular thing. And, if you don't find it, you've somehow failed at life and will never be truly happy.

What a load of old poop.

Our lives are relatively short in the great scheme of things. During our lifetime, we will have the chance to do lots and lots of things. Some of these will be really important, to both you and those around you, and some of them will be incredibly unimportant. It's the important things that we feel give our life meaning, and help us to feel happy. The unimportant things? Filler. This can be stuff that's not great, but just because it's not important, doesn't mean it has to all be awful stuff. You get a hazelnut chocolate spread that fills your sandwiches, and that stuff is what dreams are made of!

Anyway, rather than asking that huge, capitalised, neon question of: 'What is my life purpose?' what we should be asking is, 'What can I do with the time I have that is important?' Still a big question obviously, but one that has far less stress-filled parameters than our first swing at the ball. Plus, this new question has the added bonus of being proactive. Focusing on what your life purpose may or may not be hardly instils any kind of movement from you; not until you figure out what that purpose actually is. Hell's bells, you could ponder it for *years* without moving your bum off the sofa! Throw in some active contemplations into the mix by considering what you can **do** and the game changes *big time*.

There are some considerations that can help you figure that out. By the by, I'm aware of how serious a topic this can be; you're literally trying to figure out how you want to spend a huge chunk of your time here. But please, please, please, try to approach this with a sense of curiosity and light-heartedness. Making it into something heavy and overly serious could lead you to a path that is as equally weighted down. We're trying to find your happiness here, people! Even if your passions are in an area that is seen as being serious, such as medicine or law, that doesn't mean you have to have the same energy 24/7 – you are allowed to smile and be happy, you know! Even the most important areas of our lives need some happiness. In fact, they are the ones that need them the most! Just something to bear in mind...

Okay so, first off, let me tell you that, even when you do find things to do with your time here that are important and filled with enough happiness to fill a million balloons, that doesn't mean every second spent engaged in that activity is going to be a happy one.

'Woah, missy! I thought you just told me to lighten up! Why are you raining on my parade before I've even got started?'

I'm not, I swear. I just want you to realise that even the most joy-filled and fulfilling activities come with an element of sacrifice. Nothing can be uplifting all the time, no matter how awesome it is. The writer who receives a hundred rejection letters before they get their break. The high-profile lawyer who has to work an 80-hour week. The entrepreneur who faces countless failures before they find that golden nugget of an idea. If you're not willing to face the hard parts of the role, then you may fall at the first hurdle.

So, what sacrifice or struggle would you be willing to tolerate? What rough patch would you be able to handle if it meant doing something you love? The trick is to find something you're so passionate about that those difficult parts aren't your obstacle; they're just another part of it. When you do something you love, sacrifices and struggles are all worth it.

Be aware too of pinning all your hopes on 'The One'; you know, that one magical thing that we're meant to be doing. Or so we think. But fixating on this outcome leads to an incredible amount of pressure and stress on our part. Not only that, thinking there's only one thing that's meant for us actually limits us from fulfilling our greatness. Right now, I am a psychic, angel worker, magazine contributor, author and speaker – each of which brings me incredible amounts of joy. They are all aspects of my purpose; like some great sparkly mirror ball. Each role is a little mirror, and each one adds up to create my overall purpose. Life purpose isn't a singular thing; it's a complex and multifaceted operation.

There are two people in life you should seek to impress: your 80-year-old self and your 8-year-old self. The 80-year-old version of you should be able to look back at your life and smile. They should feel proud of everything you've accomplished, not just in terms of money and success, but living a life that was full of experiences and happiness. A life that was full and truly wonderful. And the 8-year-old?

When I was a girl, my whole world was books. If I wasn't reading, I was writing. Words and stories were the things that made my heart sing with joy, and I loved them. I didn't do it for praise or any kind of accolades. I didn't do it to make money, or to be somebody. I did it because I loved it and it made me really happy. As I got older though and life got in the way, I seemed to do less. It became a hobby that I did when I had the time, if and when I managed to finish the humongous to-do list that was always by my side. I lost touch with my joy.

We all have this knack of letting our childhood happiness slip through our fingers. But, just because the world sees us as adults, doesn't mean that little girl or boy isn't still within us, and wants you to continue doing the things that you used to love so much. The world puts more and more pressures on us as we grow, and it seems almost fanciful to do something for the pure joy of it. We're taught that the only things worth doing are the things we get rewarded for. Indeed, it wasn't until I was in my early thirties that I really remembered just how much I loved to write; and thank goodness I reconnected with my passion, or you wouldn't be reading this book!

If I had told my child self that I had stopped writing because I didn't think I was very good at it, or that I worried I'd never make money from it, she would sob with disappointment. She wrote because it made her happy, and happiness should be your primary motivator in every choice you make in life; especially the big sparkly ones.

Speaking of motivators: who's your biggest competition? Is it the famous writer/sportsperson/actor/musician/etc. whom you idolise? Is it the countless social media accounts you follow, all dedicated to the same interests you have? Is it your cousin who your mum keeps dropping not-so-subtle hints about, all centred on how well they're doing?

Nah. You know who your biggest competition should be?

You.

You should want to be the best version of yourself that you can possibly be; even better than the person you were yesterday. And that means loving something so much that all normal routines fly out of the window. You know what I mean – the times when you're so deeply engrossed in what you're doing that you forget to eat, that kind of thing!

Did you ever have that? I've read such amazing books that hours have gone by whilst I've been immersed in their pages. Hours where I've done nothing but read and turn pages. I mean, I'm not the type of woman who skips meals, but to be that engrossed in something shows a real enthralment that other activities may not give you. It doesn't have to be reading, clearly, but you will have at least one thing in your life that you can lose yourself in. This, in turn, could point the way to the important things you could be spending your time on.

When I started writing as an adult, I wasn't very good. That does pain me to say it, but you shouldn't hide the truth; especially from yourself. Before *Happiness: Make Your Soul Smile*, I self-published two books – *Chasing Rainbows* and *Little White Feathers*. Now, I'm not about to sit here and drive myself into some pity party or hate-heavy cul-de-sac; that's uncomfortable for you to read, and will make me feel like crap. I wrote my first book whilst I was caring for my baby twins, predominantly on my own. The urge to write was so great, that I would grab every spare moment I had to put pen to paper; no matter how tired I was. To finish the book and self-publish it is a huge accomplishment that I am really proud of myself for. But...

I have looked at *Chasing Rainbows* since and, although I see my heart behind my words, it's not the best thing I've ever written. But that's okay! If you want to get really good at something and engage in important things that make you happy, then you have to be prepared to be the bad one in the room. And being bad at anything is really embarrassing, so most people avoid it like a bad dose of the plague! However, if you never allowed yourself to potentially feel embarrassed, then you could be missing out on that all-important thing that you've been waiting for!

There are like a million reasons you could throw my way why you don't run towards your dreams like your pants are on fire. Some of them will be good and valid reasons (like missing out on spending valuable time with your children), but most come from a fear of what others may say or think about you, and that you'll look like an idiot.

Poop, poop, and more poop.

You are literally robbing yourself of being happy because you're too busy worrying about what others think, when the majority of people are too concerned with their own lives to be overly worried about yours. And those who have a vested interest in you, like your family, will have opinions because they love you. Let them see that you're happy, and their concerns will fade faster than free beer at a music festival.

Worrying about embarrassment, and letting it run your life, is like you digging a ten-foot hole and sticking your head in it. You are missing out on your life! The important things in life tend to have unique labels stamped all over them, and that means going against that sheep mentality of doing what everyone else is doing. Yes, it's scary. Yes, you've got to be brave. But the more something fills you full with fear and potential embarrassment, the greater chance it has of being something you need to jump on board with.

The world is a proper scary place right now. Pick up any newspaper, click on any website, or turn on the TV, and you'll be pretty much guaranteed to be faced with fear, panic and negativity. So, if you really want to spend your time doing something important that leaves you feeling fulfilled and happy, choose an issue and help make it better. Whether it's the environmental crisis, government corruption, famine, the poor distribution of wealth and resources between the developed and developing countries, sex trafficking, or mental health care, there's a plethora of problems to get on board with. And, clearly, you're not going to solve the problem by yourself, but that shouldn't stop you making a difference. Indeed, that feeling of knowing that you're helping and making a difference is the thing that will ultimately give you a deep sense of both fulfilment and happiness.

Let me ask you a question: if money wasn't an issue for you (let's say you won a quadruple rollover on the Lottery), what would you do with your time?

Most of us get stuck on the complacent hamster wheel of earning money. The routine of your life can sap all the joy out of you, if you're not careful. So many say, *'Well, if I knew what my passion was, I'd start doing that! But I don't have time to find it because I'm too busy working.'*

Now wait just a cotton-picking minute!

Passion is the result of action, not the cause of it.

If you want to find out what does fill you full of so much passion that it's practically bursting out of you, then you actually have to **do** things. I know, crazy right?

So, what would you do with your time if you didn't have to worry about money? Or if someone forced you out of the house every day with a gun to your head? Social media procrastination doesn't count by the way. Unless you're some tech genius and creating a new platform *is* your passion, wasting time scrolling, liking, following and commenting isn't going to get you very far. It's just another hamster wheel to get lost on. Same for television watching and video game playing. I'm talking about being out in the real world with real people, and you are going to choose something to fill your time. Something that could potentially give you bucket loads of passion.

Maybe you could take an art class Perhaps you might head off to college or university to improve yourself. You might feel called to join in with environmental protests and conservation work. Or maybe you'll knit hats for ducks. And not everything you try is going to give you that amazing sense of passion and joy, but some of them will, and you won't know unless you get out there and give things a try.

By that token, what if I told you that you were going to die in 12 months' time? I'm sorry to get morbid on you, I know that many people don't like talking about death, let alone even thinking about it. And yet, death is a natural part of life that's going to happen to us all, and thinking about it gives you a real sense of clarity. It helps you to consider what the important things are in your life, and which are simply wasting time.

So, what will people say about you once you've gone? What is your legacy? What would the obituary say?

And no, I don't think, *'She watched every show on Netflix,'* counts as true life purpose. Sorry.

If you're suddenly panicked that there is nothing to say, then what would you *like* it to say? You can start working on that today; making your legacy a reality.

You have the power to find your purpose in life. You do that by thinking how you can fill your time up with important things; by being proactive and making things happen; and following your passions. When you start to do that, you will ultimately find fulfilment and true happiness.

The two most important days in your life are the day you were born, and the day you find out why.
Mark Twain

This journey called life will be over before you realise it. Why spend another second living a life that doesn't fill you full of meaning, happiness and fulfilment?

Today I will
be happier
than a dog on
a trampoline
covered in
balloons

Big Pants Up: Invisible Crown On

So, there it is my lovelies! I have taken you on a whistle-stop tour of how to be happier in your life. On the way we've encountered everything from things we should do more of, like kindness and gratitude, and things we should definitely give up (basically anything that springs up from fear). My hope is that, through reading this book, you will feel inspired and empowered to make your happiness a priority, and that you understand that you have the power within you to make it happen. Let's run through a quick summary of the main points for you to take away in your own life. After all, there wouldn't be an awful lot of point to all of this if you simply read it and then put it on your bookshelf; the lessons learnt dismissed the second the last page was turned. This book is full of applied knowledge – I want you all to be a million billion times happier than you are now!

1. Happiness is a choice.
You can't control the things that are happening around you, but you always have the choice of how you react to them. Yes, having an abundant and secure life makes it easier to be happy, but that doesn't automatically mean you will be. Neither is it anyone else's responsibility to make you happy. You don't have to wait for their approval or permission to bring more happiness into your life. Happiness comes from within you! This is your life and you are responsible for your own happiness in every second of every day.

2. You can be happy… right now!
Please, please, please don't put your happiness off one single second longer. You have the power to start to be happier whenever you want to, and all you have to do is decide to be so. Write on a piece of paper:

I decide I want to be happy. From now on I'm going to be a happy person, no matter what.

Make sure you put it up somewhere you'll see it several times a day, like your kitchen or bathroom. You have to keep reminding yourself that you deserve to be happy, and can start to be happier right now. It's not enough to say, 'I would like to be happy' or 'I wish to be happy.' These are magical possibilities that you don't really believe in; they aren't taking you where you want to be.

And, once you've made the firm decision to be happier no matter what, you'll find that it becomes your default setting. Look, I'm not saying that this simple practice will magically make all of life's problems disappear. Life will still get pretty crappy at times, and downright bloody awful at others. But, by committing to being happy every day, you will always come back to this central place. Things and people may try to knock you off balance and pull you down into fear, but you'll find that you'll get really stubborn with it! You have chosen happiness; it's what you want, what you know you deserve, and you're not prepared to settle for anything less than that anymore.

3. Happiness is a state of being.
We live in a goal-focused society. So many of us want to know where you want to be in five years. Or what you want to be when you grow up. Results, targets and goal setting are highly valued commodities now, and you're almost seen as having something wrong with you if you don't have these as part of your dominant thinking. Focusing on the things you'd like to achieve isn't in itself a bad thing, but it may have a negative effect on how you think about your happiness. Listing your goals could almost give the impression that, until you've ticked them off, you're not allowed to be happy. But your life is happening right now in this very moment, and you deserve to be happy right now. It shouldn't matter if you've ticked off every goal on your list, if you're only

on the first step, or if you haven't even got a list! Happiness is not dependent on results and outcomes; it's your innate birthright.

4. Happiness is a choice... but so is sadness.
Life can be tougher than a piece of beef that's been boiled for a week. Stresses and worries around money, work, relationships, children and health can be a huge headache, and you may find yourself in a victim/martyr/proper fed-up mindset. When we get caught up in a daily grind of stress, your happiness can seem like a distant memory. You may wonder how you're even going to be happy again. All you keep doing is focusing again and again on how hard things are, and how unhappy you are. A great barbed stick of misery that you keep beating yourself up with!

But if you can choose to be happy, then you can also choose to be miserable. I'm not saying that your life circumstances aren't difficult, and I'm not saying that you're not allowed to be sad, angry or resentful. Your emotions are a natural reaction to each moment, and can provide valuable clues to what's going on within you. But when you're getting stuck in that place for huge periods of time, then you have to worry whether it's the situation that's causing you to feel that way, or whether you're (consciously or subconsciously) choosing to feel that way. Your life is centred on free will, and you have the power to choose in each moment what to do and how to feel. You're not a powerless victim, even if others try to convince you that you are. Take back control! You are not a tree after all; if you don't like where you are, move to something better!

5. Spread happiness around like chocolate spread on toast.
Happiness is hard to fully grasp if you try to keep it yourself. Like a slippery eel, the harder you try to keep it to yourself, the more it wants to slide out of your hands. By seeking to share it with others from an open heart, you will make others happy and yourself! Seek not to be greedy or selfish – for that shows that you don't really

believe you're worthy or deserving of being happy. The more you give, the more you will receive.

6. Happiness sometimes means making tough choices.
Nothing good in life ever came easy; and happiness is no exception. Happiness is something you have to commit to, every single day. And that means that sometimes you have to make decisions that aren't lovely or easy. For example, say you're in an abusive relationship. As hard as it will be, with support you can break free for your own peace of mind and happiness. Or your workplace is leaving you unfulfilled and deeply unhappy. Although there are risks from leaving, and you'll feel scared, there's a better future waiting out there for you.

7. Remember happiness is a marathon, not a sprint.
Happiness is a choice that takes less than a second to get on board with, but working on it takes an entire lifetime. Take it slow and try not to rush to some magical destination; it's the journey here that's the truly important thing. Your happiness is a lifelong path for you to walk upon. Mistakes are going to happen along that road, and you shouldn't allow that to stop you moving forward to a happier life. Each mistake is a lesson for you to learn from, and to help you do better next time. Don't let anything or anyone stop you being where you want to be.

8. Happiness is individual to you.
What makes me happy isn't necessarily what's going to make you happy, and that's okay. We all have our own tastes, interests, likes, dislikes and passions. If we all liked the same thing, think how dull the world would be! There isn't one way or the right way to be happy, and what I've offered in this book are the things that have worked for me. Try them, keep what works for you, and dismiss what doesn't (it's okay, I won't cry). There isn't a specific formula that everyone should follow to be happy, or a secret recipe on

the back of every milk carton (although that would be awesome). Happiness is personal and subjective. You don't need to justify your happiness to others, you just need to listen to the bang of your own drum. After all, there is a lot of power in realising that we are in charge of our own happiness. No one else gets to call the shots. And while our friends and family can be a part of our 'happiness team', they don't get to decide how to play the game or what that game even looks like. The best cheering section is the one that will cheer you on no matter what, so long as you are ultimately happier in the long run.

9. Don't be afraid of the shadows.
We all have shadows in our lives; they're a natural part of who we are. If we stay with our faces to the smiley, positive, and socially acceptable parts of our nature, we're denying all of who we are. And, by pushing down the darker side of who we are, we could potentially cause big problems for ourselves later on down the track. Sometimes we're not smiley and happy people, and that's nothing to be ashamed of. It's okay not to be okay; just don't unpack and live there.

10. You deserve to be happy.

If you take one thing away after reading this book, it's that. Let me repeat it one more time for you so it fully sinks in:

YOU DESERVE TO BE HAPPY!

Yes, really! I don't care who you are, what you look like, where you're from, or what you do. I don't care about the mistakes you've made in the past, or if you're totally clueless about where you're going next. No matter what, you deserve to be happy. And you have everything you need within you to make that your reality; if you want it bad enough.

Yes, life can be tough. Yes, bloody awful things happen in the world. Yes, it can feel damn near impossible at times to even smile, let alone be truly happy. But… it's yours for the taking *if* and *when* you're ready to grab it with both hands.

Enough with the excuses.

Enough with the procrastinating.

Enough with giving people your power.

Enough with letting fear run the show.

Enough with hating yourself.

Enough now.

Things to give up **RIGHT NOW!**

- The need for approval
- The need to impress others
- The need to always be right
- Obsessing on your past
- Being resistant to change
- Negative self-talk
- Limiting beliefs
- Blaming others
- Complaining

Instead, we are going to start doing these things, because I promise you they are going to make you feel a hell of a lot happier from the get go:

1. Accept the things you can't change. If there are things you can and you want to, then get on with it.
2. Let go of anyone who is holding you down. You know who I'm talking about, and so do you…
3. Stick on your all-time favourite song as loud as you dare to go. Sing your heart out and shake your booty!
4. Exercise as much as you can for as long as you can. You'll

get a huge boost of endorphins, which is the feel-good chemical in the brain, or you'll be so knackered that your problems won't seem so big any more.

5. Call someone you love. Texting, messaging and emailing are one thing, but hearing the voice of someone you care about can be the ultimate mood booster.

6. Smile at a stranger as you walk past them. I don't mean you need to inanely grin at everyone like a deranged idiot, but sharing a pleasant nanosecond with someone will make you both feel better.

7. Give someone a compliment. There's always something positive to say to someone else. We're so quick to moan and judge that receiving a compliment out of the blue, especially from someone who doesn't know you, is a wonderful surprise. It'll make them smile, and your heart will be extra sparkly all day.

8. Write down all the things you don't like about yourself. Rip the paper up, stamp on the pieces, burn the paper, then dunk the ashes in water! You don't need that kind of negativity in your life.

9. Put on your favourite film. Even if you've seen it a hundred times and know the entire script. In fact, especially if you've seen it a hundred times and know the entire script!

10. Stand in front of the mirror and tell your reflection, 'I love you.' Yes, you'll feel like a prize idiot, but no one needs to see you do it. We are our own worst critics, and it's all such an utter waste of time and energy. If we spent just half the amount of time loving ourselves as we do criticising, we'd all be walking around in our very own happy-filled love bubble. You are fantabulous, lovely!

This is YOUR LIFE! It's happening *right now*! What are you waiting for? Go out there and start living a life of happiness today; don't waste another precious second. I'll be cheering you on every step of the way!

Happiness Pledge

Let's finish the book with a promise to ourselves; a vow to bring more happiness into our lives. Think of it is doing a pinkie promise with yourself that you'll make your happiness a priority from now on. This isn't a document to be taken lightly, for it has the potential to change your life! Once you commit to being happy, you'll find that anything that isn't aligned with this will start to fall away – either by itself or because you won't want it anymore. So, it's not the easiest pledge in the world, but it is life changing. By promising yourself that you will start to move towards your happiness, you're starting off on one of the best journeys you've ever taken.

Ready?

Read the pledge below, and sign and date it when you're ready:

Happiness Pledge

I, _____
am ready to commit to being happier in every area of my life. Starting today, and every day, I will make happiness, joy and peace my priority. Happiness is my top priority and number one intention in every moment.

Happiness is an offset of the most powerful energies in the Universe: love. I recognise and accept that love is who I am; it is the core essence of my being. It is the Source of where I originate from, the mission of life, and where I will return. By walking the path of happiness, I allow myself to choose love in every moment. It brings untold benefits to my life, and to those around me, and to the whole planet.

I am _____ and I will no longer give my power to negative thoughts or feelings, and allow them to rob me of my happiness. I choose instead to focus on what I am grateful for, and all the good things that are in my life. I will not hide from happiness, nor feel ashamed or embarrassed of it. I choose to make it the core of my life and, in doing so, I will send out love and positivity to the whole world.

I promise to be a happiness light in the world. I will be more positively contagious, by sharing more smiles, laughter, joy and encouragement with everyone I come into contact with.

When faced with pessimism, I will choose optimism.

When faced with fear, I will choose love.

When faced with hatred, I will choose compassion.

When faced with negativity, I will choose happiness.

If I find myself faced with challenges, I will see them for opportunities to learn and grow.

My best days are ahead of me, and I commit to making them as truly happy as they can possibly be. I know that happiness and positivity makes my life better, and the lifts the whole world. I strive to make my happiness a priority, and will do all I can to make it happen; for I deserve nothing less.

My name is _____

and I pledge to be happy.

Signed: _____

Date: _____

BOOKS

O-BOOKS

SPIRITUALITY

O is a symbol of the world, of oneness and unity; this eye
represents knowledge and insight. We publish titles on general
spirituality and living a spiritual life. We aim to inform and help
you on your own journey in this life.
If you have enjoyed this book, why not tell other readers by
posting a review on your preferred book site?

Recent bestsellers from O-Books are:

Heart of Tantric Sex
Diana Richardson
Revealing Eastern secrets of deep love and intimacy to Western couples.
Paperback: 978-1-90381-637-0 ebook: 978-1-84694-637-0

Crystal Prescriptions
The A-Z guide to over 1,200 symptoms and their healing crystals
Judy Hall
The first in the popular series of six books, this handy little guide is packed as tight as a pill-bottle with crystal remedies for ailments.
Paperback: 978-1-90504-740-6 ebook: 978-1-84694-629-5

Take Me To Truth
Undoing the Ego
Nouk Sanchez, Tomas Vieira
The best-selling step-by-step book on shedding the Ego, using the teachings of A Course In Miracles.
Paperback: 978-1-84694-050-7 ebook: 978-1-84694-654-7

The 7 Myths about Love...Actually!
The journey from your HEAD to the HEART of your SOUL
Mike George
Smashes all the myths about LOVE.
Paperback: 978-1-84694-288-4 ebook: 978-1-84694-682-0

The Holy Spirit's Interpretation of the New Testament
A course in Understanding and Acceptance
Regina Dawn Akers
Following on from the strength of *A Course In Miracles*, NTI teaches us how to experience the love and oneness of God.
Paperback: 978-1-84694-085-9 ebook: 978-1-78099-083-5

The Message of A Course In Miracles
A translation of the text in plain language
Elizabeth A. Cronkhite
A translation of *A Course in Miracles* into plain, everyday language for anyone seeking inner peace. The companion volume, *Practicing A Course In Miracles*, offers practical lessons and mentoring.
Paperback: 978-1-84694-319-5 ebook: 978-1-84694-642-4

Rising in Love
My Wild and Crazy Ride to Here and Now, with Amma, the Hugging Saint
Ram Das Batchelder
Rising in Love conveys an author's extraordinary journey of spiritual awakening with the Guru, Amma.
Paperback: 978-1-78279-687-9 ebook: 978-1-78279-686-2

Thinker's Guide to God
Peter Vardy
An introduction to key issues in the philosophy of religion.
Paperback: 978-1-90381-622-6

Your Simple Path
Find happiness in every step
Ian Tucker
A guide to helping us reconnect with what is really important in our lives.
Paperback: 978-1-78279-349-6 ebook: 978-1-78279-348-9

365 Days of Wisdom
Daily Messages To Inspire You Through The Year
Dadi Janki
Daily messages which cool the mind, warm the heart and guide you along your journey.

Paperback: 978-1-84694-863-3 ebook: 978-1-84694-864-0

Body of Wisdom
Women's Spiritual Power and How it Serves
Hilary Hart
Bringing together the dreams and experiences of women across
the world with today's most visionary spiritual teachers.
Paperback: 978-1-78099-696-7 ebook: 978-1-78099-695-0

Dying to Be Free
From Enforced Secrecy to Near Death to True Transformation
Hannah Robinson
After an unexpected accident and near-death experience, Hannah
Robinson found herself radically transforming her life, while a
remarkable new insight altered her relationship with her father; a
practising Catholic priest.
Paperback: 978-1-78535-254-6 ebook: 978-1-78535-255-3

The Ecology of the Soul
A Manual of Peace, Power and Personal Growth for Real People
in the Real World
Aidan Walker
Balance your own inner Ecology of the Soul to regain your
natural state of peace, power and wellbeing.
Paperback: 978-1-78279-850-7 ebook: 978-1-78279-849-1

Not I, Not other than I
The Life and Teachings of Russel Williams
Steve Taylor, Russel Williams
The miraculous life and inspiring teachings of one of the World's
greatest living Sages.
Paperback: 978-1-78279-729-6 ebook: 978-1-78279-728-9

On the Other Side of Love
A Woman's Unconventional Journey Towards Wisdom
Muriel Maufroy
When life has lost all meaning, what do you do?
Paperback: 978-1-78535-281-2 ebook: 978-1-78535-282-9

Practicing A Course In Miracles
A Translation of the Workbook in Plain Language and With
Mentoring Notes
Elizabeth A. Cronkhite
The practical second and third volumes of The Plain-Language *A
Course In Miracles*.
Paperback: 978-1-84694-403-1 ebook: 978-1-78099-072-9

Quantum Bliss
The Quantum Mechanics of Happiness, Abundance, and Health
George S. Mentz
Quantum Bliss is the breakthrough summary of success and
spirituality secrets that customers have been waiting for.
Paperback: 978-1-78535-203-4 ebook: 978-1-78535-204-1

The Upside Down Mountain
Mags MacKean
A must-read for anyone weary of chasing success and happiness
– one woman's inspirational journey swapping the uphill slog for
the downhill slope.
Paperback: 978-1-78535-171-6 ebook: 978-1-78535-172-3

Your Personal Tuning Fork
The Endocrine System
Deborah Bates
Discover your body's health secret, the endocrine system, and
'twang' your way to sustainable health!
Paperback: 978-1-84694-503-8 ebook: 978-1-78099-697-4

Readers of ebooks can buy or view any of these bestsellers by clicking on the live link in the title. Most titles are published in paperback and as an ebook. Paperbacks are available in traditional bookshops. Both print and ebook formats are available online.

Find more titles and sign up to our readers' newsletter at http://www.johnhuntpublishing.com/mind-body-spirit

Follow us on Facebook at https://www.facebook.com/OBooks/ and Twitter at https://twitter.com/obooks